MARCO

Travel with Insider Tips

KOS

BULGARIA — Black Sea

MAC — Thessaloniki — İstanbul

ALBA-NIA

Athens — TURKEY

GREECE

Kos — Rhodes

Crete — CYPRUS

Mediterranean Sea

LIBYA — EGYPT

www.marcopolouk.com

SYMBOLS

INSIDER TIP   Insider Tip

★   Highlight

●●●●   Best of ...

☼   Scenic view

☺   Responsible travel: for eco-
     logical or fair trade aspects

(*)   Telephone numbers
       that are not toll-free

PRICE CATEGORIES
HOTELS

Expensive	over 80 euros
Moderate	50–80 euros
Budget	under 50 euros

Prices for two people
in a double room per night
without breakfast in high
season

PRICE CATEGORIES
RESTAURANTS

Expensive	over 15 euros
Moderate	12–15 euros
Budget	under 12 euros

Prices for a meal consisting
of a meat dish, potatoes,
a Greek salad and 1/4 bottle
of wine

On the cover: Ágios Stéfanos Basilica p. 72 | Bubble Beach p. 79

CONTENTS

The West → p. 70

Trips & tours → p. 80

Sports & activities → p. 86

Road atlas → p. 108

MAPS IN THE GUIDEBOOK
(110 A1) Page numbers and coordinates refer to the road atlas
(0) Site/address located off the map. Coordinates are also given for places that are not marked on the road atlas
(U A1) Refers to the map of Kos town inside the back cover

**INSIDE BACK COVER:
PULL-OUT MAP →**

PULL-OUT MAP 𝄞
(𝄞 A–B 2–3) Refers to the removable pull-out map
(𝄞 a–b 2–3) Refers to additional inset maps on the pull-out map

The best MARCO POLO Insider Tips

Our top 15 Insider Tips

INSIDER TIP **Design and sea**
Only a narrow beach separates the Kos Aktís hotel from the waves of the Aegean Sea. Gaze on the ocean and the mountains of the Asia Minor coast from the comfort of your bed → p. 47

INSIDER TIP **'Beautiful Greece' ...**
... is the translation for the traditional 'I Oréa Elláda' farm house. A Flemish lady has converted it into a restaurant, selling paintings and renting out two apartments as well → p. 69

INSIDER TIP **Sweet things from two worlds**
Many Koans reckon the Parádosi bakery to be the best on the island. The owners belong to the Muslim minority and create delicious tarts, home-made ice cream and excellent Oriental pastries → p. 43

INSIDER TIP **On a mule's back**
Instead of clambering up to the Café Ória, patrons may also place their trust in a mule → p. 64

INSIDER TIP **More than souvenirs**
Pia and Ira use their shop to sell pretty jewellery and souvenirs, but also look after the animals on the island, arranging dog sponsorships or flights back with tourists → p. 60

INSIDER TIP **Dance in the Turkish baths**
Clubbing at the Hamam Club means dancing in former Turkish baths between natural walls and under a dome painted with murals (photo left) → p. 46

INSIDER TIP **True hospitality**
Guests staying at the small Afendoúlis hotel are welcomed so warmly that they soon feel part of the family → p. 46

INSIDER TIP **Zorbas open air**
Consistently beautiful summers lure Hollywood stars outside too: you can watch them appear every evening on the screen of the Cine Orféas in the original version → p. 46

INSIDERTIP Just dive in

The Liámis Dive Centre offers trydive courses in safe coves as well as adventurous trips to wrecks and into sea caves → p. 88

INSIDERTIP Ride on

The trek rides offered near Old Pýli run on trails through the mountains of the island → p. 92

INSIDERTIP Climbing with sea views

Those in the know appreciate the island of Kálimnos as one of the best climbing areas in Europe. Near-unique in the world: the immediate proximity of the climbing zones to the sea (photo right) → p. 87

INSIDERTIP Bubble Beach

The popular Paradise Beach harbours a secret that only reveals itself to snorkellers – this is the way to discover its bubbly underworld → p. 79

INSIDERTIP Under the leaf canopy

Hidden away, the village square of Mandráki on Níssiros is one of the most beautiful in the Aegean. Sit under the canopy of huge rubber trees and enjoy a succulent kid goat that fed on the aromatic herbs from pastures on the slope of the volcano → p. 83

INSIDERTIP Slow Food – Koan style

In the cosy Mary's House restaurant a bit off the beaten track, your host María still takes her time cooking and baking, putting rarely offered Greek dishes onto the limited menu and looking after her select number of guests with a lot of passion → p. 43

INSIDERTIP Farmer on the beach

With no tavern to be found anywhere nearby, a farming family from Kéfalos treats its guests to products from the region. Enjoy typically Greek cuisine – a stone's throw from the beach → p. 73

BEST OF ...

FOR FREE

● *Music of the spheres beneath the theatre*

At the catacombs of the Roman theatre, spherical background music is an important part of the exhibition concept (photo left) → p. 40

● *Mythological picture-book*

The mosaics in Kos' western excavation zone are free storytellers. Find out how the European continent got its name, and watch gladiators fight → p. 41

● *Forage for your souvenirs*

Take a trip to Níssiros and collect pumice stones on the tiny local beach of Mandráki → p. 83

● *Scrap metal art*

In the Neptune Resort between Mastichári and Marmári, an artist has recreated deities and heroic figures from Greek mythology, as rusty sculptures → p. 59

● *Gallantry and romance*

Anybody may climb the walls of Antimáchia castle to enjoy the spectacular panoramic view. And the wilderness inside, populated by countless lizards, is a real experience → p. 53

● *Picnic in the forest*

Not all Koans rush to the beach on summer Sundays. Families and young couples also like to head for the small forest of Pláka. The large picnic area sees a lot of barbecuing, eating, drinking and even some dancing sometimes. Forest walks and expensive beach entertainment is left to the tourists → p. 94

● *Spa with a difference*

At Embrós Thérme thermal water, heated to a temperature of 45 °C/112 °F, flows into the sea. In an improvised pool between the rocks you will find mostly Greeks taking a free thermal bath → p. 51

●●●● Dots in guidebook refer to 'Best of ...' tips

● *Truly public*

Life on Kos is lived far more in the public eye than at home. If you needed proof, visit the kafeníon in the town's court building where the curious may follow court proceedings through the open doors with a cup of mocha in their hand → p. 42

● *Ottoman cuisine*

Kos is the only Greek island apart from Rhodes where Muslims originally from Turkey still have their home. They show their culinary skills in the tavernas on the village squares, nearly all bearing Turkish names. Whether cooked or grilled dishes: the spicy secrets of Asia Minor are an experience for the palate → p. 44

● *Cows on the beach*

On Kos, cows are nearly as omnipresent as in India. You find them in the countryside, on the beach or in the odd quiet alleyway. This is the only place in Hellas you will see this – and between Tigáki and Mastichári is Cow Central → p. 65

● *Making new friends*

The old farmers living right next to the ancient tomb of Harmylos in Pýli are often to be found sitting outside the small church waiting to chat to visitors and pamper them with water or fruit – hospitality Koan-style → p. 62

● *Old times*

If you want to see how older Koans lived when they were children, visit the Traditional House in Antimáchia, erected and furnished following historic models: cosy it might have been, though not very comfortable for sure. The attraction also shows how tourism has changed the island (photo right) → p. 52

● *Pick a picnic*

The small Koan churches located outside the villages usually have an area reserved for festivities with long tables and benches. This is where after the service on the church feast day the locals eat, drink and party together. This square at the Ágios Ioánnis Pródromos monastery near Kéfalosis truly idyllic → p. 77

ONLY IN

BEST OF ...

AND IF IT RAINS?
Activities to brighten your day

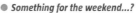

● *Something for the weekend...?*
The bawdy allusions in the sculptures on display in the Archaeological Museum work in any weather: just look at the statue of a god decorated with bull's testicles... → S. 36

● *Rain or shine ...*
... the merchants in the shop-lined alleyways of Odós Iféstou und Odós Apéllou are open for business. Dozens of shops offer their wares to those fleeing the rain drops → p. 44

● *Painting with Sol*
Artist Sol offers painting courses for young and old. If the weather is not playing ball, they take place in the studio or in a café → p. 63

● *Roman luxury*
For an impressive and lively idea of the comfort that rich Romans enjoyed, go to the restored Casa Romana. The walls were colourfully painted, the floors laid out with mosaics, and thermal baths awaited next door → p. 37

● *Arabian Nights*
Most restaurants on Kos are at their best in good weather, but the charms of the Hamám Oriental lie inside, across two floors of former Turkish baths → p. 42

● *Close to heaven*
Prettily painted inside, Orthodox churches are usually open all day long. The priest in the church of Lagoúdi enjoys talking to visitors → p. 69

● *Culinary souvenirs*
First and foremost, Kos' historic market hall serves to provide shade; however, on rainy days it offers a welcome roof too. Here you will find small gastronomic presents from all over Greece for little money (photo left) → p. 44

CHILL OUT

● *Hammocks and saffron water*
There's always a relaxed atmosphere at Olympia Mare apartment house. Hammocks dangle between tamarisk trees, sun loungers await in the shade, and occasionally the grande dame of the house will serve some saffron-flavoured water → **p. 56**

● *Sunset spectacular*
Many visitors rush to the mountain village of Zía to witness its breathtaking sunsets. A much more romantic spot for appreciating this natural spectacle far from the hustle and bustle is around places such as Ágios Theológos → **p. 75**

● *Dune tune*
The relaxed lounge music playing in the background tunes you in to the laid-back style of the dune restaurant Tam Tam. On a fabulously green lawn the guests sit right above the sandy beach, while at the back Koan cows graze stoically → **p. 60**

● *Sweet and salty*
The spa area of the Kos Imperial Thalasso hotel is as luxurious as the place itself. Alongside various saunas, an Ayurvedic centre and hydrotherapy pool, a huge area with seawater and freshwater pools in different sizes awaits (photo right) → **p. 47**

● *Yoga in the Pántheon*
A British operator organises one to two week yoga courses in the Hotel Pántheon. Classes are held in English, and it is also possible to take part just for the day → **p. 89**

● *Magnetism*
Travellers' reports often talk about the special aura they have felt around the ancient theatre near Kéfalos → **p. 75**

● *Sunbathing under full sail*
How about chartering a sailing yacht with crew just for the day? The route is determined by the wind and yourself → **p. 89**

INTRODUCTION

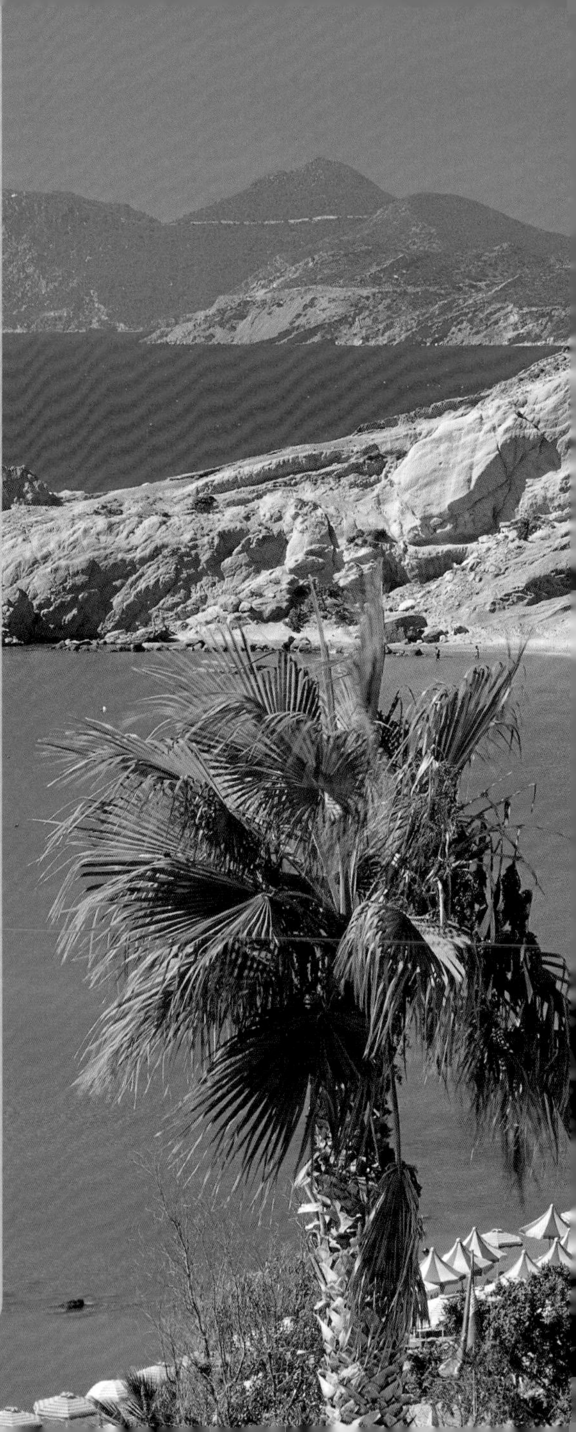

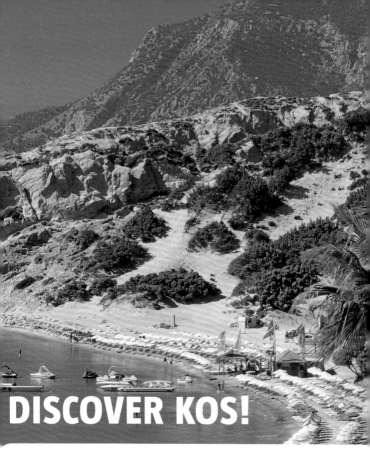

DISCOVER KOS!

Aegean winds usually blow from the north – which is why planes start their landing approach level with the sponge diver island of Kálimnos and then fly in a wide curve leading past the volcanic island of Níssiros to the airport. Seen from the air, Kos reveals itself as an elongated island, 30 miles long and no more than 6 miles wide. This means no house or hotel is far from the sea, lined by miles and miles of beaches that are clearly visible from the air.

The airport is situated more or less at the exact centre of the island. A long flat mountain crest runs through the island, from the mountainous Kéfalos peninsula in the west to the Díkeos mountain range in the east. Thanks to the excellent central road traversing the island, a transfer from the airport to any hotel never takes longer than 40 minutes. So the plane has hardly touched down and you're on holiday. Kos Town, the tranquil capital of the island, is home to well over half of the island's 31,000 inhabitants. The rest are spread over a handful of larger villages, with only Kéfalos situated over to the west of the island. Tourism is the only really important economic

Photo: Paradise Beach at Kéfalos

An ancient sports facility: remnants of the gymnasion in Kos Town

sector. There is no industry, and agriculture is mainly restricted to the cultivation of grain and keeping cows or sheep. In the ranking of most popular Greek destinations, Kos occupies number four, behind Crete, Rhodes and Corfu. A main reason for this are the many all-inclusive hotels and club complexes such as Robinson and Magic Life, where large international tour operators ensure permanently high rates of occupancy.

On Kos, eco trends were recognised early on

Koans know exactly how important the tourists are for the island and do a lot to keep their guests happy. Identifying and implementing ecological trends early on, Kos has been promoting bike use for years. As practically all holiday areas and beach hotels are situated in the flat coastal plain on the northern coast between Mastichári and Ágios Fókas, using a bike requires no great effort. Wide cycle

2000–1450 BC
Minoan culture on Crete

1600–1150 BC
Mycenaean culture

1150–750 BC
Kos is settled by the Dorians, a Greek tribe

750–490 BC
Archaic era, emergence of the Greek city states

490–336 BC
Classical era. In 460 a doctor called Hippocrates is born on Kos

336–82 BC
Hellenistic era. Kos is governed by the Egyptian Ptolemies

paths and roads with little traffic run parallel to the sea, making the bike an ideal mode of transport. Children and visitors who are not used to cycling can join in and enjoy this way of getting around, which stimulates all the senses. Sometimes paths cut across grain fields that are harvested as early as May and then used as cow pastures or to cultivate melons. Others lead along low dunes, calling passers-by for an impromptu swim. And again and again you'll discover shady groves of trees right by the sea, perfect for a short rest. Many taverns along the way have installed bike stands – you'll be hard-pressed to find a Greek holiday region that is as bike-friendly as Kos. Only hikers still baffle the Koans. That somebody would walk when they don't have to is still a mystery to them, so sign-posted and maintained hiking trails are the exception on Kos.

Another exemplary initiative is the public transport network. Town bus lines connect the surrounding beach hotels with the capital until late at night, overland buses link the capital with villages and beaches. This means getting around doesn't have to involve spending much money or polluting the atmosphere. Even take-away copies of bus timetables are available, something practically unheard-of in other parts of Greece. Within the town area the bus stops have numbers, meaning you don't have to memorise complicated names and may step onto your bus relaxed and with Mediterranean serenity.

Talking of which, a certain serenity is a fundamental characteristic of most Koans. A mad rush is alien to them. This is visible in the cafés, where statistically they make a single cup of coffee last 94 minutes, and in the taverns where they lavishly dine

82 BC–395 AD
Kos forms part of the Roman Empire

395–1307
Kos belongs to the East Roman Byzantine Empire

1307–1523
The Knights of St John occupy the Dodecanese

1523
The Turks conquer the Dodecanese

1821–29
Greek struggle for independence, foundation of a new independent Greek state, encompassing at first only the southern Greek mainland, the Cyclades and the Northern Sporades

the night away. Koans would never consider going on an English-style pub crawl or moving from one tapas bar to the next like the Spanish. Too much moving around would hinder their chats with friends – and that to the Greeks is what going out is

94 minutes for a cup of coffee

about first and foremost. Nor do the locals want to keep trying new places, preferring instead taverns and cafés where the owner knows them. As a visitor you soon experience the warm feeling of being treated like a regular, even if it's only the second time they see you. For the hosts, this is less about increasing their turnover than about the appreciation afforded to them: if a guest comes back, it means that they must be doing something right. Most Hellenes hold up their honour, filótimo, as one of the highest goods in life, which is why it is also not accepted to criticise others. Not saying anything positive is judgement enough.

The natural environment of Kos is not spectacular as such, but surprisingly green and varied. At an altitude of 2775 ft, the Díkeos mountain range, while dropping off steeply and inaccessibly towards the southern coast, doesn't stand comparison with the wild mountains that dominate the mainland or Crete. After rainy winters and far into the spring, hundreds of flamingos visit the saline lake of Tigáki. In the narrow erosion valleys in the centre of the island, field flowers and wild artichokes can blossom without being disturbed. And on the green Kéfalos peninsula sheep find a lot of space for grazing. Here, holidaymakers can hike for hours and will only meet a few farmers or shepherds. The near-treeless landscape allows the gaze to wander far across the land, so that despite the lack of signposting nobody gets lost. The only time it gets lonelier still on Kos is between mid-October and early May, when the vast majority of tourists have left. During that period, companies that live off tourism stay closed, and many Koans choose to do some travelling themselves. Those staying at home look after the family and the olive trees, as their fruits fall to the ground between November and March and have to be picked up as quickly as possible so as not to lose quality.

The island's most famous son is from Kéfalos in the quiet west of the island: Hippocrates. Born in 460 BC, he is considered the 'father of medicine'. On Kos Hippocrates founded a medical school that lasted for nearly 1000 years. Looking at illnesses no longer as trials sent by the gods, he researched their sources, which

1912
Italy conquers the Dodecanese

1947
The Dodecanese become part of Greece

1967–1974
Military dictatorship and abolition of the monarchy

1981
Greece becomes a member of the EU

2004
Greece hosts the Summer Olympic Games

2010/11
International financial aid keeps the Greek state from bankruptcy

Koan beach life: not only humans like to soak up the sun

he often found in environmental conditions and the lifestyle of his patients. Hippocrates would observe his patients closely and saw his main job in strengthening their powers of self-healing. Giving nutritional advice, Hippocrates prescribed natural medicines, but also found a clever way to involve the gods in his therapies, interpreting the dreams of his patients as divine counsel, helping to trigger psychosomatic processes of self-healing. Hippocrates' teaching was so successful that following his death the Asklípion was erected in his honour, turning Kos into one of the largest centres of healing in the ancient world. This most important historical site of the island can be found on the edge of Kos Town. Even those travelling to Kos just for sun and sea should not miss this unique mix of temple complex and hospital, in a spot with beautiful views to boot.

When Hippocrates reinvented medicine

The number of testimonies to the Hellenistic and Roman periods on Kos is fairly limited – unlike the number of sunshine hours. Between June and August hardly a single raindrop falls, temperatures climb above the 30° C/85 °F mark on a daily basis, and the sea is pleasantly warm. That is when Kos can play its biggest tourist trump, the superb sandy beaches that announced the island from aboard the plane. Whether above or below, in the water or on the water's edge: this is paradise for both active travellers and sunseekers.

WHAT'S HOT

1 Trendsetters on the rocks

It's Boulder Time When climbing in Greece is mentioned, Kos' small neighbouring island of Kálimnos that springs to mind first of all. But it is Kos itself that boasts probably the most recent, but at the same time largest and best bouldering area in the country, the *Hippocrates Boulders*. Here, you climb with views of the adjacent sea. The well accessible small and large blocks of rock are granite and have everything from overhangs to gaps to squeeze through. Some 200 routes lead through them, well marked and of different levels of difficulty *(turn left 200 m before you reach the Mitsis Norída Beach hotel)*. Books on the subject are available too. The obvious choice to stay the night is the *Mitsis Norída Beach* hotel, as the Hippocrates Boulders are only a few minutes away *(Kardámena, www.mitsishotels.com)*.

Party time with a twist

Dance the night away When the sun kisses the west of the island goodnight, nightlife in the east is already well under way. Every evening Kos Town and the legendary bar mile of Odós Pléssa turn into a single party strip, allegedly with the highest club density in Greece! From sunset to dawn, visitors and locals use the warm night to really push the boat out. The hotspot for night owls is the *West Bar*, where the party goes on both inside and in the fresh air at outdoor tables and chairs *(www.west.gr, photo)*. In *Kyttaro*, try a round of Beer Pong. It's a lot of fun, not as smelly as it sounds, and there are even championships in this boozy variation on table tennis. The emblem of the *Wild Bull Bar* is a red bull on the wall. Guests party hard here; sooner or later they're all dancing on the tables *(www.wildbullbar.gr)*.

Colourful festivals

In the thick of it Kos doesn't like to conform to the cliché of 'remote island'. International festivals bring cosmopolitan flair to the small isle. Each September for instance to honour Hippocrates, the father of modern medicine and idol of ancient Greek doctors, who was born on the island, the *Kos Ippokratis International Health Film Festival* takes place. A professional audience and visitors watch contributions on the subject of health and illness prevention; the best and most creative ideas receive awards *(www.healthfilmfestival.gr, photo)*. On the musical front, Kos also plays in the international league. After its successful premiere in 2009, every summer sees the *International Philharmonic Orchestra Festival* with ensembles from all over the world, with an emphasis on brass instruments *(www.kos.gr/politismos/ekdilosis)*.

3

KOS ippokratis
3RD INTERNATIONAL HEALTH FILM FESTIVAL

Kaneláda

4

From traditional drink to party cocktail Kaneláda has been a popular souvenir for a while. Now, mixed with water and ice, but also with cola and spirits, the cinnamon beverage is turning into a party drink in bars and pubs. This sweet traditional drink originally hails from the neighbouring island of Níssiros, where it is still produced today and sold in Mandráki in the *Paradosiakó* shop. You can taste *kaneláda* freshly prepared as a digestif in the *Iríni* restaurant *(Platía Ilikiomenis, Mandráki)*. On Kos itself, gourmets can find the cinnamon mixture bottled on the beaches off the main square of Zía: add ice and soda water, and enjoy this Greek invention!

IN A NUTSHELL

AGÍA, ÁGII, ÁGIOS

On Greek islands you will constantly come across these three words. They form part of place names and church names and also appear in the names of fishing boats and car ferries. *Agía* means saint (female), *Ágios* saint (male), and *Ágii* is the plural of both. The Virgin Mary is called *Panagía*, the All Holy.

ALL-INCLUSIVE

These days, over 60 per cent of all hotel beds on Kos form part of all-inclusive resorts. Visitors love this kind of holiday, and it has brought above-average rates of bed occupancy to Kos. However, many Greeks are demanding a ban on this system, which they call *clubs*. As the tourists' money is mostly spent in the resorts, some cafés and taverns in the tourist centres have had to close or only yield minimum profits now. All-inclusive creates only low-level local employment; in the face of these large-scale outfits, chances for Koans to establish successful tourist operations are slim.

ANCIENT GODS

To the ancient Greeks, the gods were omnipresent, interfering in wars and day-to-day life, having affairs with mortals and demanding to be honoured by humans the way they should. Their most important ritual sites were the temples. Later, the Romans took on most of the Greek gods, giving them Latin names. As the latter are usually more widely known than the Greek names, we will here give

Understand Kos better – life on this little island is different way to what you know from home

the Roman deity names in brackets. Zeus (Jupiter) was considered the most powerful god. His wife was Hera (Juno), whose main sanctuary was located on the island of Sámos. She was the protector of marriage. Zeus' brothers were the sea god Poseidon (Neptune) und Hades (Pluto), the god of the underworld. A son of Zeus and Hera, Hephaestus (Vulcan) was the god of blacksmithing and jewellers. His wife Aphrodite (Venus) was the goddess of love; her own lover was the war god Ares (Mars). Zeus' extramarital affair resulted in Apollo, the god of beauty, light and healing. His twin sister was Artemis (Diana), the goddess of hunting. Dionysos (Bacchus) finally was the god of fertility, wine and theatre and is still venerated fervently today.

CRISIS

In 2011, the state of Greece was facing bankruptcy. The European Union and International Monetary Fund helped out with credit guarantees and through buying state bonds, but demanded drastic savings measures in return. By 2014, annual borrowing will have to be lowered from 14 to 3 per cent of GDP. The debt crisis had many sources: an inflated civil service, lack of tax discipline, superannuated industries, but also corruption promoted by foreign companies and a level of nepotism worthy of the old Ottoman Empire. Kos has felt the austerity measures in lower occupancy rates from Greek holidaymakers and lower turnover in tourism in general. Now, Koans place big hopes on their Turkish neighbours: since 2010, they no longer need a visa, so that increasingly you see Turkish yachts entering Kos marina, and many more day trippers coming over from Bodrum.

DODECANESE

Kos belongs to the Dodecanese archipelago, one of over 50 Greek administrative regions. Its Greek name *Dodekaníssia* means 'twelve islands'. In reality the Dodecanese include 19 inhabited islands. Most of them lie in the string of islands along the Turkish coast from Pátmos via Rhodes all the way to the minuscule island of Kastellórizo half way between Rhodes and Cyprus. The regional government works out of Rhodes.

ENVIRONMENT

When it comes to protecting the environment, Koans are streets ahead of the rest of Greece, keeping their island remarkably clean. The water treatment plant in the east appears a flowering paradise, burning of refuse takes place underground, so that there are no more smouldering fires out in the open. In

Icons are used by believers to communicate with the saints

terms of recycling, too, Kos is an example to many other Greek regions. While there aren't yet any household recycling facilities, Koans increasingly divide up paper, glass, plastics and metal themselves and take them to the collection points.

FAUNA & FLORA

Kos has no large wild mammals, and even encounters with snakes are rare. The animals seen most often are lizards, which can reach up to 20 cm. The plant world presents much more diversity. The northern slopes of Mount Díkeos have preserved a few conifer forests, and many dunes are covered with juniper. The most common tree planted along avenues is the eucalyptus, while springs, fountains and brooks are shaded by plane trees. On the sandy beaches, the typical tree is the tender tamarisk, also called salt tree for its tolerance of salt. In spring and early summer, streets and mountain slopes show flowering gorse, while streets and brooks display vivid growths of oleander. Popular decorative plants on house walls and in gardens are bougainvillea and hibiscus. Unusual fruit trees include the light-red flowering pomegranate tree and the medlar tree which in spring bears yellow fruit with a somewhat acidic but very refreshing taste. Kos is particularly rich in flowers between February and May, when meadows and pastures sprout countless flowers that have been all but eradicated elsewhere by pesticides: poppies and the calla lily, wild tulips and anemones. A characteristic of the phrygana, a kind of low-growing macchia landscape, are many aromatic herbs such as thyme, lavender and sage.

FUTURE

2011 marked the start of a reform of Greek municipal structures that bears the name of the ancient architect of the Acropolis, 'Kallíkratis'. This reform is turning the entire island into one administrative entity. The new mayor is promoting sustainable tourism. Climbing routes and mountain bike pistes are being developed in the Díkeos mountain range, the saline lake of Alikí is being opened up for ecotourism. New parks are planned, as well as special support for local agriculture, husbandry and apiculture. Now all that remains is for the election promises to be followed by actions.

GENERATIONAL PROBLEM

On Kos, members of the younger generation have a big problem: they are overqualified. Too many parents have invested a lot of money in their children's academic education, with too few suitable jobs available on the island. The young generation have no other choice but to either move to the mainland conurbations around Athens, Thessaloníki and Patras – or to temp in the summer as waiters or taxi drivers on their home island in order to at least qualify for job-seekers' allowance in the remainder of the year.

ICONS

In the Orthodox church, representations of saints and biblical events on panels are called icons. Icons are very different from the pious images in our churches, they are 'gateways to heaven' bringing the saint into the house, making him or her present. The eyes, nearly always facing the viewer head on, create the pathway through which the spirit of the believer enters into contact with what is represented. As consulates of heaven on earth, as it were, icons enjoy a high degree of veneration, being treated as if they were the saints themselves. The representation of the saints and the saints themselves are held to be one and the same in essence. Panajótis Katapódis, for example, has been manufacturing icons for churches, but also for private clients and tourists, since 1962. From choosing the wood and applying the gilt down to wielding the paintbrush, he does everything himself. His work in churches gave him the idea to produce framed fresco fragments as decorations for the home. You may watch the artist at work and place your own order for an icon. His Swedish wife Kristína speaks good English (studio in the suburb of Ágios Nektários north of town, look for the signpost saying 'Icon Painter' at the small car park east of Casa Romana; but make sure to call in advance: *tel. 22 42 02 49 42*).

KAMÁKI

Travelling on your own, ladies? On Kos this doesn't have to stay that way for long, thanks to the *kamákia* (the literal translation yields something like 'harpoons'). Always very well dressed and with a golden necklace adorning a half-exposed chest, they are able to start a conversation in many of the world's languages. Many of them are waiters or souvenir sellers in their day job. In fairness it should be said that they are not just after scoring notches on the bedpost: a number of *kamáki* have ended up the husband of a foreign lady.

KIOSKS

Kiosks, in Greek called *períptero* in the singular, stand on every square and in towns and villages at many larger crossroads. Usually open every day of the week from early in the morning to late at night, they peddle everything and anything that clients might need: newspapers and magazines, cigarettes and disposable razors, toothbrushes and combs, single aspirins, condoms and much more.

MIGRATION

Having seen much emigration of its own people up to 1980, Greece has become a country of net immigration since 1990. The largest group of migrants on Kos are the Albanians, who are by now well integrated and work mainly in construction and agriculture. Many of them have brought their families over to live with them. There are also quite a few Bulgarians and Romanians, most of them working as day labourers and seasonal workers in hotels and restaurants.

MILITARY

Due to the proximity to Turkey, numerous soldiers are stationed on Kos, without however spoiling the holiday feeling in any way. While both nations have been members of the Nato military alliance since 1952, the historic enemy right outside the front door is still mistrusted. The high military presence demands a high defence budget, contributing to the country's economic problems.

POLITICAL PARTIES

As elsewhere in Greece, two parties dominate the political landscape on Kos. Due to a lack of local authority funds, local politicians have little political power – nearly everything is decided in Athens, where the conservative Néa Dimokratía under the leadership of Kóstas Karamanlís governed for a long time. The October 2009 elections were carried by the social-democratic PASOK party led by Jórgos Papandréou. Both parties bear a major share of the blame for Greece's financial crisis. Following every election new low-level civil service posts for party supporters were created, without suppressing others. This led to an enormous inflation of the well-paid civil servant sector. Many posts were filled several times over. Consequently, those civil servants had little to do, leaving them free to take early retirement – costs that weigh heavily on the state's finances.

RELIGION

Apart from a small Muslim minority on the islands of Kos and Rhodes and in Western Thrace on the mainland, as well as small Jewish communities in the big cities, nearly all Greeks profess allegiance to Greek-Orthodox Christianity.

Everywhere on the islands you meet the Orthodox priests. Their Greek name is *pappádes* (singular: *pappás)*. Orthodox priests are allowed to marry before entering the priesthood and often have large families. They are paid by the state; there is no church tax in Greece.

All priests improve their income through fees for weddings, baptisms, etc.; many work as farmers too.

Orthodox services often last two hours or more. Few churchgoers last that long, so that there is a constant toing and froing. The main content of the service are the formal antiphony chants performed by the priest and some laymen.

Orthodox Christians don't accept the pope in Rome as the head of Christianity, holding this claim to be the devil's work. Having developed their belief system from early Christendom and not changed it since the 9th century, they feel a strong connection with and allegiance to the Apostles and early Christians. Orthodox Christians categorically refute the god-given character of the dogmas proclaimed by the Roman Catholic pope while also decrying the work of the Protestant reformers.

Chapel on Díkeos mountain

FOOD & DRINK

Greek eating habits differ strongly from ours. There are a good number of restaurants on Kos that have adapted to Western European style and taste, though many taverns still cultivate Hellenic culinary customs.

The Greek love their *mezedákia*, placing various small dishes on as many plates as possible on the table at the same time. In the evenings Koans would hardly ever go out to dinner on their own. For them the fellowship of a happy table, *paréa*, is as important as culinary enjoyment. A *paréa* is always about ordering different dishes that are placed in the centre of the table, so everybody can take what and how much they like. Usually, meat and fish are also served on large platters to be enjoyed together. These Greek hab-

its explain why many waiters in taverns and restaurants don't really understand the idea of a menu sequence, usually bringing first courses and main courses practically at the same time. Usually a *paréa* would order a lot more than they can eat: to devour everything is seen as embarrassing, showing that obviously not enough food has been ordered. All plates, even the empty ones, would usually stay on the table. Waiters don't clear the table so the *paréa* can see at all times how well they have feasted.

The Greeks prefer to have the waiter list what the kitchen has to offer on the day and to discuss the finer points. Menus are practically always multilingual, and in tourist hotspots often illustrated with photographs. When they arrive, the dish-

Mezedákia instead of a set menu – Koans love culinary variety spread across many plates, and like to share their meals with others

es usually look completely different from the pictures, which are often taken in a professional photo studio rather than in the kitchens of the individual tavernas.

One custom that is not just Greek but widespread in Mediterranean countries, means that nearly all restaurants and taverns add a small cover charge to the bill. The amount can vary between 0.20 and 4 euros. In some eateries waiters will now ask foreign guests whether they'd like bread. If you say no, you don't pay the cover charge.

Famous Greek specialities such as *moussaká* and *souvláki* appear on most menus. More unusual Greek dishes are worth trying too, though. While you don't have to go for grilled lamb's head, *kefalákia*, or tripe soup, *patsá*, chick-pea puree, *fáva*, or fish egg puree, *taramá*, are great culinary discoveries. A more rare delicious find are *anthoús*, courgette flowers filled with rice and herbs. An excellent Hellenic alternative to the Greek farm salad is *chórta*, a salad from cooked wild plants such as chard, dandelion or coltsfoot leaves.

LOCAL SPECIALITIES

▶ **ádana kebáb** – grilled mincemeat, well seasoned, and served optionally with dried chili

▶ **bakaljáros me skordaljá** – dried hake (merluza), served with a potato-garlic puree

▶ **békri mezé** – pork goulash in a sauce with finely chopped peppers

▶ **briám** – a kind of ratatouille made with different vegetables, usually including courgettes and aubergines

▶ **fakí** – lentil soup, eaten on Good Friday as a national dish

▶ **juvétsi** – oven-baked noodles (looking a bit like rice) with beef (sometimes lamb)

▶ **kokorétsi** – innards stuffed into a natural gut casing and grilled on the skewer

▶ **kolokithósupa** – pumpkin soup

▶ **lukanikópitta** – puff pastry filled with a frankfurter-type sausage (photo left)

▶ **marídes** – crisply fried anchovies fried, eaten with head and tail

▶ **patsá** – tripe soup, a favourite after a night spent partying or at an early-morning market

▶ **patsária** – beetroot, served cold as a salad or lukewarm including the leaves as a vegetable

▶ **revithókeftédes** – a kind of pancake made with chickpea flour

▶ **soumáda** – refreshing drink made from almond milk and water

▶ **spanakópitta** – puff pastry case filled with spinach

▶ **stifádo** – beef or rabbit goulash with Spanish onions in a tomato-cinnamon sauce

▶ **taramosaláta** – a reddish puree made from potatoes or soaked bread and fish roe, a popular first appetiser

▶ **tirópitta** – puff pastry case filled with cheese

Nearly all restaurants and taverns are open all day long. Often English breakfast is served from 10 o'clock onwards; main meals can be had at any time really between 11am and midnight. For a small snack or on days when you want to save some money, small snack restaurants called *psistaría* offer a good alternative to the restaurant. Visitors with a sweet tooth will want to head for a Greek pastry bakery, *zacharoplastío*, serving mainly Oriental specialities alongside cream tarts and sand cakes. Make sure you take advantage if you see *loukoumádes* on offer: always freshly deep-fried in oil, these doughnuts are enjoyed sprinkled with honey and cinnamon or icing sugar. The Greek national drink is water. Some places still serve free iced tap water with coffee or dinner. Not much wine is sold by the glass on Kos, while there is a wide range of fine wines from small wineries. The Koan 😊 *Oinampelos Winery* even produces an organic wine from the Greek Malagoúsia grape and the internationally known Sauvignon Blanc grapes. Retsína, resinated white wine, is also produced on Kos.

In terms of alcohol, the Greek national drink is *oúzo*, an aniseed liqueur, which is taken either neat, on ice or mixed with water. The best Greek *oúzo* brands are said to be distilled at Plomári on the island of Chíos further north, i.e. *Plomarioú, Mini* and *Barbayiannis*. Another after-dinner pick-me-up is *Metaxá* brandy, available in various qualities.

The Greeks drink coffee all day long, on any occasion. Ordering coffee in Greece however is a near-scientific endeavour. To start with there is the choice between Greek mocha, *kafé ellinikó*; hot instant coffee, usually called *ness sestó*; and cold instant coffee beaten to a froth and served with ice cubes, *frappé*. Also, don't forget to state the degree of sweetness you'd like, as the water is boiled together with the coffee powder and sugar: *skétto*, no sugar; *métrio*, with a little sugar; *glikó*, with a lot of sugar. Greek coffee is always drunk without milk. If you'd like your hot or cold Nescafé with milk, add the words *me gála*. The same applies to cold fashionable drinks such as *freddo espresso* or *freddo cappuccino*, appreciated mainly by younger consumers.

A terrace in the shade: a good start for lunch

SHOPPING

Apart from gold and silver jewellery, a few hand-painted icons, sponges cut from the bottom of the sea or gastronomic treats made by small artisan operations, the range of authentic souvenirs is not exactly huge. You'll find the biggest selection in Kos Town and the small 'artists village' of Pýli. In the capital many products were made in Greece if not in Kos itself. A much bigger selection of souvenirs can be found in Bodrum in Turkey, with products from all parts of that country. With bigger items such as carpets you are better off having them sent directly back home.

ART

The only good place to find authentic art on the island is the village of Pýli.

FASHION & SHOES

For fashionable clothes, most Koans go to Rhodes or straight to Athens. Kos doesn't offer a wide selection, and has nothing really in the upper price segment. This doesn't mean you can't make some good fashion discoveries. Take a stroll through the shops along the Odós Venizélou and Odós Xanthoú, keeping an eye out for the shoe shops with extravagant Greek footwear fashions.

GASTRONOMY

Koan wine is a simple table wine. If you're looking for good Greek wine you will find it in the market hall in Kos Town and in small off-licences, usually called *cáva*. Truly Koan delicacies are fruit marinated in syrup, which you can get in the market hall for instance. There you also find many specialities from other Greek regions. Thyme honey and dried herbs could well be from Kos, while the saffron on offer is not from the region, but mostly from the northern Greek town of Kozáni. If you take a trip to the neighbouring island of Níssiros, do get a small bottle each of *kaneláda* cinnamon lemonade and *soumáda* almond milk as well as the natural pumice.

MUSIC

Souvenir shops sell numerous CDs with

Art and gastronomic delights – this guide lets you sidestep tourist traps and leads to the souvenirs typical for the island

Greek music in the style of the Aléxis Sorbás film, which no Greek person would buy, relatively cheaply. If you're looking for high-quality recordings of contemporary Greek music, regardless of style, you are better off heading for the specialised shops in the island capital, where you can get advice, check out the charts and listen to the recordings. Greeks often buy pirate CDs from dubious street vendors. These might be cheap but are pressed illegally, and you can't check the quality of the recordings. Better leave those well alone!

OPENING TIMES

Shops selling groceries and day-to-day items are usually open Monday to Saturday from 8.30am to 2pm, and also on Tuesdays, Thursdays and Fridays between 6pm and 9pm. Supermarkets are open between Monday and Saturday from around 8am to 9pm. Souvenir shops are open every day, usually between 8.30am and 11pm.

SPONGES

Natural sponges are best bought from the ambulant vendors at the port of Kardámena. For an even bigger selection take a boat trip to the neighbouring sponge divers' island of Kálimnos.

SUPERMARKETS

As everywhere in Europe, on Kos too small individual shops are giving way to the large supermarket chains. The locals do their bigger shops usually in the shopping centres on the edge of town along the main road to Zipári.

THE PERFECT ROUTE

ENJOY THE MORNING AT THE ASKLÍPION

Driving through the village of **1** *Platáni* → p. 40, inhabited by both Christians and Muslims, first head for the **2** *Asklípion* → p. 48. In the balmy air of early morning, the view of the Asia Minor coast across the water is still clear. Between the exit and the car park the café owner is glad to see his first guests enjoying the morning with a coffee or freshly-squeezed orange juice.

KOAN TRADITION

Head west on the main island road to **3** *Antimáchia* → p. 52, the village in the interior of the island directly adjoining the airport. The *Traditional House* in the village centre gives an idea of how people lived in the times when there were no tourists on Kos and when flour was still ground in mills such as the one opposite.

DISCOVERIES OUT WEST

Following the call of the wild west, it's a good 10 mi to reach the next settlement: Kéfalos, stretching out into the coastal plain. Here, the ruins of the most beautiful of the island's many Early Christian basilicas stands right on the beach: **4** *Ágios Stéfanos* → p. 72. The village of **5** *Kéfalos* → p. 71 offers the chance of a coffee break before carrying on to soak up the lonely atmosphere around the abandoned monastery of **6** *Ágios Ioánnis Theológos* → p. 75. Goats and sheep graze along the wayside, sometimes a farmer might greet from atop his donkey. What is guaranteed is a fantastic view, reaching on some days all the way to the island of Mykonos. Head back via Kéfalos, stopping here at the latest for a refreshing dip in the sea, best taken on the calm **7** *Magic Beach* → p. 78.

AN OLD TOMB AND A CASTLE

Next up comes the large inland village of **8** *Pýli* → p. 62. Here you will find the tomb of Harmylos, which not only holds much archaeological interest, but enjoys a very idyllic location too. The 400-year-old village fountain awakens nostalgic feelings in the shade of an enormous ficus tree. Two galleries might entice you to consider some shopping (photo to left) – and the wild romantic ruined castle of **9** *Old Pýli* → p. 63 is worth

the brief detour. A little fitness is required here, as the way to the castle leads uphill through the forest for some ten minutes.

SURPRISES IN THE SMALL VILLAGE OF LAGOÚDI

To make up for this, the tiny village of ⑩ *Lagoúdi* → p. 69 then offers pure relaxation. In the village church with its pretty murals, the Orthodox priest enjoys chatting to visitors. At *Oréa Elláda* your hostess Christina cooks up culinary delights. Attached to her café is a gallery with antiques from the island, select yet affordable jewellery and art works by the Flemish owner.

FANTASTIC SUNSET AT ZÍA'S

The nearby mountain village of ⑪ *Zía* → p. 66 is so famous for its beautiful sunsets that every late afternoon numerous buses slog their way up there. If you want to escape the masses, hike through the village past an old watermill up to the *Sunset Balcony* restaurant and watch from there as the sun goes down into the sea or behind the neighbouring island of Kálymnos (photo right).

TAKE A NIGHT DIP

The car has been hired for 24 hours. Why not get the most out of it? If you are up for a very special experience, go for a swim in the warm seawater of ⑫ *Embrós Thérme* → p. 51, where a healing thermal spring joins the Aegean. A torch helps with this little nocturnal adventure.

68 miles. Driving time 3 hours without breaks. Detailed map of the route on the back cover, in the road atlas and the pull-out map

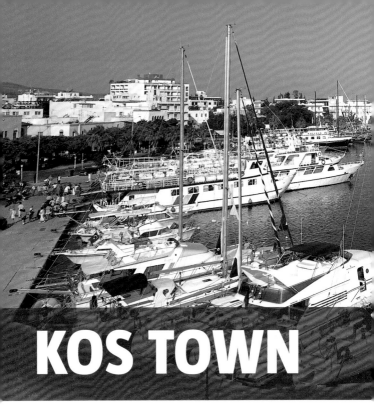

KOS TOWN

⬛⬛⬛ MAP INSIDE THE BACK COVER
Kos (115 D2) (*K1–2*) boasts one of the most beautiful locations of any Aegean town. Embedded in lush green, it is situated right on the ocean, with the Díkeos mountain range as a backdrop, rising up steeply to the south behind gentle slopes.

Across the water the gaze settles onto the Turkish coastline opposite, which, depending on the weather, sometimes appears near enough to touch, and at other times can only be made out as a silhouette. The core of the town (pop. 18,000) is formed by the circular *Mandráki* port, used by yachts and fishing boats, pleasure steamers and coastguard boats.

Immediately behind the shore promenade lies the town centre with its shopping streets and small squares, mosques and ancient ruins. To the east, the port meets an extensive medieval castle, with the flags of Greece and Europe blowing in the wind, as if to signal to the Turks on the other side that Europe starts on Kos.

> ### 🏙 WHERE TO START?
> Get off the local bus at the terminus at **Aktí Miaoúli (U D4)** (*d4*), only a few steps from the Plane Tree of Hippocrates. The terminus for the long-distance buses is only three minutes from the market hall. If travelling by car, the best place to park is in the car park east of the Casa Romana.

Photo: Mandráki Harbour

In a very compact area, the capital unites architectural testimonies to various cultures, spanning three millennia

At the point of the small peninsula where the castle was erected, car ferries, catamarans and hydrofoil boats come and go. On the other side of the port you'll nearly always see a freighter moored, delivering cement and other construction materials.

To the west of the harbour lies the *Lambí* hotel and tourist quarter with its many restaurants, clubs and service facilities. The area reaches to the island's winery and beyond and is fringed by miles of sandy beaches. East of the castle another

hotel quarter begins by the beach and merges into the loosely built-up suburb of *Psalídi* with its large hotel resorts. Holidaymakers will pass much quieter nights here than in the Lambí quarter.

The particular charm of Kos town centre lies in the way it is a tapestry of buildings from different centuries and millennia, that aren't fenced off, museum-style, but may be explored at any time, day or night. Any stroll turns into a time-travel experience between classical antiquity, the medieval era and contemporary

Exactly how the Agorá looked like in antiquity can only be guessed at today

times, with their individual cultures. Southwest of the centre, the former village of Platáni these days belongs to Kos Town. Here, Muslims of Turkish origin and Christian Greeks live together as they did in Ottoman times. While Platáni offers no holiday accommodation, you will find food that cannot be found anywhere else in Greece. From Platáni, a cypress-fringed avenue leads to the Asklípion, the island's most important archaeological site. In antiquity people from the entire Mediterranean made a pilgrimage here in the hope of being healed from their ailments. Today, the excavation zone still resembles the park of a spa.

SIGHTSEEING

AGORÁ (U D4) (*m d4*)

The ancient market square of the town is a very romantic field of ruins, though not particularly easy to decipher. The origins of the Agorá go back as far as the 4th century BC. In medieval times the houses of the Knights of St John stood on this area, covering some 180 x 80 m. While still inhabited in the times of Turkish dominion, it was razed to the ground by an earthquake on 23 April 1933. The quake reached 8.5 on the Richter scale, lasted only 27 seconds and killed 170 people. Italian archaeologists were able to bring out the bright side: the disaster meant that they were allowed to have the medieval ruined houses torn down and start looking for the traces of antiquity further below. In so doing, they found the remains of a long colonnade with shops, pinpointed today by two uprighted pillars. Corinthian capitals mark the place of a sanctuary dedicated to Aphrodite. In the east of the area, traces of an Early Christian basilica can be made out. The southwestern corner still features part of a medieval defensive tower; magnificent bougainvilleas twine up the *Toll Gate*, though which you reach Odós Nafklírou from Platía Eleftherías. The gate probably owes its name to the fact that medieval merchants wanting to sell their wares in Kos had to pay a toll here. *Freely accessible at all times | between Odós Nafklírou, Odós Ippókratous, Platía Eleftherías and Defterdar Mosque*

ALEXANDER ALTAR (U C4) *(ᗰ c4)*
When Macedonia, part of the former Yugoslav republic, became independent in the early 1990s, and some hotheads there all of a sudden were laying claim to the Greek metropolis of Thessaloniki, Greece was shaken by a storm of outrage. *Macedonia is Greek* was the slogan – not devoid of a certain truth – that suddenly popped up everywhere in the country. The Macedonian king Alexander the Great was roped in to give substance to this statement. In the last third of the 4th century BC he conquered large parts of the civilised world as it was known at the time, advancing as far as India. The purpose was to show that he had been no Slav but a Greek. Everywhere in the country saw the erection of new Alexander monuments. The very simple and modest affair here on Kos is amongst the best, showing Alexander the warrior who slaughtered many people, not as a hero, bur rather quoting an extract from one of his speeches, ironically the one where he calls the peoples of the Earth to eternal peace. The Greek text has been

MARCO POLO HIGHLIGHTS

The floor mosaic 'Welcoming Asklípios' – a treasure from Roman times

translated into three languages – English, French and German – so that everybody can form their own opinion on Alexander's thoughts. *Freely accessible | Odós Tsaldári/Odós El. Venizélou*

ARCHAEOLOGICAL MUSEUM ●
(U C4) *(ഥ c4)*

Erected in 1936, under Italian occupation still, the building presents its collections across six rooms. To see them you need a good half hour.

Starting from the entrance, the best thing to do is to proceed directly into the inner courtyard of the museum, the *atrium*. Here, you are standing right in front of the first highlight of the circuit: a colourful *floor mosaic* dating from the 3rd century, i.e. from Roman times. In a section of the image framed by plant tendrils you can see a bearded man leaving a boat and placing his left foot on to a narrow jetty. On land, he is greeted by a simply dressed man with a hat and stick. The left-hand corner of the mosaic shows a seated bearded man wrapped in a white garment in front of a rock. This is the doctor Hippocrates receiving the visit of Asklípios, the god of healing. The man greeting them is a passing peasant. The atrium holds several *Roman statues* too. Not pretty as such but impressive is the group of figures in a near-baroque style: the naked god Dionysus, drunk, is holding an empty wine goblet in one hand. With the other he is leaning on a vine stock crowned by the god of shepherds, Pan, recognisable by his goat's feet, short horns and pan flute. With his right arm, the feminine-looking Dionysus is leaning on a satyr, an inebriated young man from his retinue. Sitting at their feet, a small Eros, the personification of eroticism, is caressing a wild animal. The work has been dated back to the 2nd or 3rd century.

From the atrium, walking counter-clockwise through the inner rooms of the mu-a closer look. The largest is kept under a modern protective roof on the northern edge of the excavation zone. A frieze full of amusing representations of wild animals runs around a rectangular image showing the Judgement of Páris (see below).

Two further  entertaining mosaics await at the eastern end of the excavation zone below smaller protective roofs at their original site. The gladiators represented here must have been as popular as professional footballers today, as they are even named in inscriptions: Aigialos, Zephyros and Ylas. The mosaic shows the half-naked Zephyros with a trident and short sword in his hands fighting Ylas, wearing helmet, shield and breastplate. The second mosaic explains how a continent got its name: Zeus has fallen in love with the young Phoenician princess Europa. Changing into the shape of a white bull, Zeus carries her off to Crete and makes her his wife. From then on, the European continent has borne the name of this beautiful princess. The mosaic shows the scene of the abduction. A dolphin accompanies the two on their voyage across the seas, while an Eros bearing the Flame of Desire in his hand is leading the bull. *Freely accessible | north of Odós Grigoríou E'*

FOOD & DRINK

INSIDER TIP **AENÁOS** (U C4) (*m c4*)
Kafeníon run by a young crowd wedded to old traditions. Here, the Greek coffee is still boiled in hot sand rather than on an open flame, and served in the small typical long-stemmed brass jugs. This café doesn't serve any kind of alcohol, instead offering a big selection of freshly-squeezed juices. *Platía Eleftherías in the Defterdar Mosque opposite the market hall | daily | Budget*

The pillars of the gymnasion date back to the 2nd century BC

In the Old Town, stroll along the shops and restaurants lining Odós Ifaistou

AMPÁVRIS (U C5) *(ﾉﾉ c5)*

Open-air tavern in the garden of an old country house. There is no menu here, rather the host will enumerate the unusual Greek specialities on offer. *On the road beginning immediately to the west of the Casa Romana | daily, evenings only | Moderate*

CIAO (U C4) *(ﾉﾉ c4)*

Modern café in the Old Town's main street. Good selection of cakes, ice cream and snacks. With many holidaymakers strolling past, there's always some gossip to be had. *Odós Ifaistou 2 | daily | Expensive*

HAMÁM ORIENTAL ★ ● (U B5) *(ﾉﾉ b5)*

Atmospheric café by day, high-class restaurant and cocktail bar at night, housed in former Turkish baths from the 16th century, plus garden. With international and Oriental music playing in the background, enjoy Oriental and Mediterranean cuisine, choose a wine off the list or directly from the wine cellar, and smoke a shisha water pipe to round it all off. *Odós Níssirou/ Platía Diágoras | daily | Expensive*

INSIDER TIP KAFENÍON AT THE COURT BUILDING ● (U D4) *(ﾉﾉ d4)*

On the back of the imposing government offices from Italian times, turned towards the Plane of Hippocrates, you'll see the court room of the Koan district court. Access to the house is through a nameless kafeníon, whose plastic chairs also stand outside on the square next to the plane tree. When the court is in session, the door behind the café and the court room always remains wide open, so that you may observe Greek court proceedings for a few minutes without drawing attention to yourself. *Platía Platanoú | closed Sun | Budget*

OTTO E MEZZO (U C4) (*m c4*)
Fine Italian restaurant in and behind a house dating back to 1879. Excellent, freshly made pasta, wonderful sauces, extensive wine list, good service. *Odós Apelloú 21 | daily | Expensive*

INSIDER**TIP** **PARÁDOSI** (U K2) (*m k2*)
Founded in 1955, the pastry bakery owned by a family originally from Turkey is considered by many Koans as the best on the island. The selection of cakes and pastries of all kinds is enormous, extending from cream tarts and sand cakes to lightly spiced Oriental pastries such as *baklavá* and *kataïfi*. The many flavours of tasty ice-cream are also home-made. There are tables inside and outside. *Platáni, on the Platía | daily from 9am onwards | Budget*

PÉTRINO (U B4) (*m b4*)
High-class restaurant in an atmospheric stone house with a pretty terrace. Low music comes out of the loudspeakers, the waiters wear a tie. The best thing though is that you can try rare specialities here, amongst them puff pastry cases filled with spinach and cheese (*spanakotirópitta*) and octopus croquettes (*chtapodokeftédes*). Try the excellent northern Greek red wine from the little mountain town of Métsovo, 3280 ft high up: *Katógi Averóf* is rarely served on the islands. *Platía Ioánnou Theológou | closed for lunch | Expensive*

INSIDER**TIP** **PÉTRINOS MÝLOS** (U C1) (*m c1*)
Café-bar in an old windmill on Mýlos Beach in the Lambí part of town. The terrace is furnished with wooden tables and director's chairs, and the service is particularly friendly here. In the evening the terrace is illuminated by oil torches and a campfire, with a DJ spinning tracks. Lots

KONÁKI (U C2) (*m c2*)
Try this very popular grill for its tasty chicken, gyros and other Greek grill specialities. The meat comes from their own butcher's, and they also serve wine by the glass. *Odós Kanári 1 | daily | Budget*

INSIDER**TIP** **MARY'S HOUSE** (U C2) (*m c2*)
Lovingly furnished, this small restaurant offers specialities such as pork chops slow-cooked in the oven for seven hours, or *dákos*, baked aubergine with three types of cheese similar to the Italian bruschetta, and for afters *mastícha* ice cream with the unique taste of a tree resin from the island of Chíos. *Odós Averóf 80 | daily | Moderate*

NICK THE FISHERMAN (U C2) (*m c2*)
Excellent fish tavern right on one of the city's busiest roads. *Odós Averóf 21 | daily | Expensive*

of little snacks are available, of which the so-called *oúzo assortment* comes highly recommended. *Daily | Moderate*

PLATÍA OF PLATÁNI ★ ●
(114–115 C–D 2–3) *(㎝ K2)*
Any of the four taverns on the village square – *Arap Memis*, *Serif Karawesir*, *Gin's Place* and *Alis* – will serve you equally well. A typical characteristic of the Turkish-influenced cuisine that awaits you here is the addition of yoghurt to many dishes. Recommended specialities are *ádana kebab*, which guests can spice up with dried chilli as they see fit, and *anthoús*, courgette flowers filled with rice and herbs. A drink not often found in Greece, *airan* is a yoghurt drink thinned down with water, lightly salted and extremely refreshing. *All four restaurants open every day | Budget*

INSIDER TIP PSAROPOÚLA
(U C2) *(㎝ c2)*
This simple tavern scores through its good selection of reasonably priced fish and traditional dishes. One of the rare vegetarian delights, *fáva* is a puree made from yellow peas mixed with onions and olive oil. In a clay jug in the oven you can see the *revíthia stamnás* being cooked: chickpeas in a well-seasoned tomato sauce. *Odós Averóf 17 | daily | Moderate*

SPÍROS (115 E2) *(㎝ L2)*
Secluded tavern with a pretty canopy of leaves above the terrace. Often playing live Greek music on Saturday nights. *In the Psalídi part of town right on the Georgíou Papandréou coastal road, immediately west of the large Hippocrates Palace hotel | daily | Budget*

SHOPPING

The most important shopping streets in town are ● *Odós Iféstou* and the adjoining *Odós Apéllou* (U C4) *(㎝ c4)*.

INSIDER TIP ALFA GOLD (U C4) *(㎝ c4)*
Professionally managed by a German-Danish couple, who get their 30,000 various items of jewellery in from all over the world. Here you will also find a good selection of reasonably priced jewellery, even black diamonds, and special pieces for children. *Odós Ríga Feréou 9*

GATZÁKIS GOLD (U C4) *(㎝ c4)*
Theodóros Gatzákis and his wife sell a tasteful selection of modern gold jewellery. Pieces are far less opulent than is often the case in Greece. *Odós Ach. Pasanikoláki 1*

LAMBÍS PÍTTAS (U C3) *(㎝ c3)*
A good place to pick up unusual ceramics, mostly from the owners' own workshop. *Odós Kanári 6*

MARKET HALL ★ ● (U C4) *(㎝ c4)*
Built by the Italians in 1934 and now fully air-conditioned, the small market hall has no equal in terms of cleanliness and order in the whole of Greece. However, today the original range of fresh fruit and vegetables is being pushed back by ever more culinary and other souvenirs sold to holidaymakers. These days, you can buy anything from *soumáda* almond milk from the island of Rhodes or sweet pickled carrots from the northern Greek town of Kavála to herbs, sponges and shell bowls. A typically Koan proposition are sweet pickled mini tomatoes, watermelon pieces and aubergine slices *(glikó omatáki, glikó melitzanáki, glikó karpoúzi)*. It is safe to wash your fresh fruit at the fountain right inside the market hall. Pay at the tills on the exits. *Mon–Sat 7am–11pm, Sun 10am–2pm and 6.30–11pm | Platía Eleftheriás/Platía Agías Paraskevís*

NARKÍSSUS (U C4) *(🗺 c4)*
Specialised shop selling the typically Greek *távli* game (similar to backgammon) and chess. *Odós Iféstou 23*

TI AMO (U C4) *(🗺 c4)*
The selection of Greek music here is as excellent as the advice. *Odós Al. Ipsilánou 4; Odós El. Venizélou 11*

LEISURE & SPORTS

As soon as you leave the harbour basin, at each end, you find narrow sand-and-pebble beaches. In immediate proximity to the town they are always busy, and in high season really crowded. Towards Psalídi things get quieter, and the occasional meadows with trees go down all the way to the shore. Towards Lambí too, the beach becomes emptier the further

you get away from the harbour, to blend with the sandy ribbon of miles and miles of beaches along the northern coast.

ENTERTAINMENT

No other Greek island, with the exception of Mykonos, can boast nightlife as intense as that in Kos Town. The numerous clubs only empty towards dawn. A particularly high density of establishments can be found in the Old Town (U D4) *(🗺 d4)* between the Mandráki harbour and the Agorá.

FASHION CLUB (U C3) *(🗺 c3)*
Central club close to the square with the dolphin fountain, with seating inside and outside, where the music successfully drowns out the noise from the street. *Odós Kanári 2 | www.fashionkos.gr*

Unique in Greece: the market hall of Kos Town

HAMAM CLUB
(U D4) *(ᴔ d4)*

Small Turkish baths have been turned into a dance floor. The domed old stone vaults create an ambience that agrees with nostalgic and romantic souls. *Bar Street*

ORFÉAS (U E5) *(ᴔ e5)*

The municipal open-air cinema lies in an oleander garden with a bar serving small *souvláki* skewers alongside drinks. On show are mainly English-language films in the original version with Greek subtitles. *Showings: June– mid-Sept daily 8.30pm or 9pm and 10.30pm or 11pm | on the eastern town beach between harbour and marina, Odós Vas. Georgíou/Odós Fenarétis | ticket 7 euros*

WHERE TO STAY

AFENDOÚLIS ☺
(U E5) *(ᴔ e5)*

Small hotel in a quiet location east of the Old Town, near the beach. Your welcoming hosts Aléxis and Denise speak good English and have an unobtrusive way of fostering guests' contacts to each other and quickly giving them a glimpse of intact Greek family life. Both are committed to recycling and strive to use only Koan products for breakfast. Air-conditioned rooms and pick-up from the harbour on request. *23 rooms | Odós Evripídou 1 | tel. 22 42 02 53 21 | www.afendoulishotel. com | Budget*

ÁSTRON (U C3) *(ᴔ c3)*

Simple mid-range hotel on the harbour. The rooms out towards the back are quiet, while those looking out front have balconies with harbour views. Behind the house is a small swimming pool and a whirlpool bath. *75 rooms | Aktí Kountourióti 31 | tel. 22 42 02 37 03 | www. astron-hotel-kos.gr | Moderate*

DIAMOND DELUXE (U C3) *(ᴔ c3)*

Design hotel a good 3 mi west of the harbour on Lambí beach. Many of the 110 rooms and suites have direct access to the 2000 sq m pool complex, while seven of the suites (up to 60 sq m) have a private pool. The spa area too, has luxurious dimensions, at over 1000 sq m. *Néa Alikarnássos | tel. 22 42 04 88 35 | www.diamondhotel.gr | Expensive*

BOOKS & FILMS

▶ **Che Committed Suicide** – The latest case for Inspector Kóstas Charítos: if you're looking for a good page-turner offering entertaining glimpses into Greek day-to-day life and Greek mentality into the bargain, the detective novel by Athens-based author Pétros Márkaris is a sound choice. Four of the mysteries have been translated into English.

▶ **Exploring the World of the Ancient Greeks** – John Camp's and Elizabeth Fisher's 2002 publication is a concise historical study of Greek culture from the Bronze Age to the Christian era.

▶ **He Who Must Die** – Nikos Kazantzakis' 1948 novel Greek Passion was made into a movie by Jules Dassin in 1956 starring Melina Mercouri – who later went on to become Greece's first female Minister for Culture.

The illuminated Lagoon Restaurant at the Hotel Kos Imperial

GRECOTEL KOS IMPERIAL THALASSO
● (115 F3) (*M2*)
Built in the style of a small Greek town; one main building plus several bunga- lows, six pools with landscaped lagoons, hydrotherapy spa centre, tennis courts, sauna, steam room and bike rental. Varied animation programme, kids club with crèche for children from three up to twelve years old. *Psalídi, 2.5 mi east of Kos Town | tel. 22 42 02 50 30 | www. grecotel.gr | Expensive*

INSIDER TIP ▶ KOS AKTÍS
(U E4–5) (*e4–5*)
The first beach tourism hotel on Kos, built in the 1960s, was converted into a de- sign hotel in 2005. All rooms look out on to the Aegean Sea, with some even offer- ing sea views from the bathtub. On the hotel terrace – open to the public – you are practically sitting on the edge of the surf. Named after the chemical formula for water, the hotel restaurant (*open every day | Expensive*) is called 'H2O'. *48 rooms | Odós Vas. Georgíou B' 7 |* *tel. 22 42 04 72 00 | www.kosaktis.gr |* *Expensive*

OCEANIS BEACH RESORT
(115 F3) (*M2*)
Extensive hotel resort right on the beach, with two pools, tennis courts, club, wa- ter sports centre, bike rental. *356 rooms | Psalídi, east of the coastal road near Ágios Fókas | tel. 22 42 02 46 41 | www. oceanis-hotel.gr | Expensive*

SEAGULL (115 F3) (*L2*)
Only five minutes from the beach, this small apartment complex run by the Di- moúdis family stands amidst a green gar- den with different lawn areas for playing and relaxing, pool and pool bar. Prices are family-friendly and barbecue eve- nings can be organised on request. Ac- tive holidaymakers can tackle the Díkeos mountain with Mr Dimoúdis. Minimum stay seven days. *14 rooms | Psalídi, on the road to Ágios Fókas | tel. 22 42 02 25 14 | www.seagull-kos.gr | Budget*

MUNICIPAL TOURIST INFORMATION
(U C4) (🗺 c4)

Kos Tourist Organisation | Aktí Koundouriótou 7 (in the town hall at Mandráki port) | tel. 22 42 02 84 20 | www.kosinfo.gr

ÁGIOS FÓKAS (115 F3–4) (🗺 M3)
The low cape on the southeastern point of the island holds a military base. There is a quiet beach below the cape. The only large hotel in the area is the hotel and bungalow complex of *Dímitra Beach (260 rooms | tel. 22 42 02 85 81 | www.dimitrabeachhotel.com | Expensive)* with garden, pool, tennis court and bike rental. Rooms may only be booked as part of a package and on an all-inclusive basis. Right in front of the hotel is a bus stop for one of the town buses. *Just over 6 mi outside Kos Town*

LOW BUDGET

▶ The Aléxandros tavern **(U C4)** **(🗺 c4)** between the Agía Paraskeví church and Iféstou Street is always striving to have the lowest prices in town. *Odós Irakléous 6 | daily from 10am onwards*

▶ On every first Sunday in April, May, June and October, entry to the Archaeological Museum **(U C4)** **(🗺 c4)** and the Asklípion **(114 C3)** **(🗺 J2)** is free of charge. The same applies on official public holidays and on the last weekend in September, as well as on Sundays between November and March.

ASKLÍPION ★ (114 C3) (🗺 J2)
In antiquity there were sanctuaries for Asklípios, the Greek god of the healing arts, everywhere in Greater Greece. The temples and altar of the god would receive the visits of those who were urgently looking for help or respite from long-term illnesses.

Asklípios was the son of Apollo, the god of light, and the mortal Korónis. During her pregnancy, Korónis was unfaithful to Apollo, and Apollo killed her with an arrow, saving however the unborn child from her womb and giving it to Chíron the centaur to be educated. One of the subjects the centaur taught the child Asklípios was the art of healing.

While Hippocrates was alive (460–377 BC) the Asklípios sanctuary didn't exist in the form we see today. The site probably only held a small temple of Apollo and an altar for Asklípios. At the end of the 4th century BC the sanctuary was extended, receiving the form we see today between the 2nd century BC and the 2nd century AD.

The sanctuary is laid out in terraces. The lowest terrace was mainly reserved for recuperation and medical purposes. Once, several temples would have stood on the central terrace, together with a sacrificial altar and buildings used by the priests. The largest and most splendid temple, an edifice dedicated to Asklípios, would have stood here since the 2nd century BC on the uppermost terrace.

From today's entrance, a reconstructed *marble staircase* with 23 steps leads up to the first terrace, with an area of 93 x 47 m. Here, a gatehouse, the *propylon*, once adorned with four pillars, received visitors; the foundation walls can still be made out. The first terrace was surrounded by a covered walk called a *stoa*. Rising in the east since Roman times, behind the covered walk was a building holding the thermal baths. Today the south is still bounded by a long wall.

30 broad steps lead up to the central terrace; several of the most interesting pillars have been uprighted again. The two Ionic ing. An open courtyard was surrounded on three sides by colonnades in the Ionic style running along the top of a marble foundation and open towards the temple. In the centre of the courtyard stood

The Asklípion complex stretches across three levels

pillars to the right belong to the *Asklípios Temple* dating back to the early 3rd century BC. This was a so-called Antes Temple measuring 8.80 by 15 m and consisting of a square open vestibule *(pronaos)* and a closed main room *(cella)*, which was probably only accessible to priests. The *cella* has a chamber let into the floor, probably to keep the temple treasure safe. Many pilgrims gifted large sums of money to the sanctuary after being healed.

The *altar of Asklípios* east of the temple was originally a rather imposing build-

the sacrificial table for burnt offerings. Standing between the pillars of the hall were statues of Asklípios, his daughter Hygeia and other goddesses. A marble ramp led up to the courtyard, in order to make it easier to pull in the sacrificial animals. They were then sacrificed and burned on this altar. East of the altar, seven re-erected Corinthian pillars mark the outlines of a Corinthian *Temple* of *Apollo* from the 2nd/3rd century.

A reconstructed flight of 60 steps leads onto the uppermost terrace, which

The pillars of the Temple of Apollo have been placed upright again

measures 100 x 80 m. Since the 2nd century BC a *circular Doric temple* would have risen at its centre, the most magnificent of all the temples in the sanctuary and dedicated to Asklípios. The temple was surrounded by a colonnade with six columns each on the narrow sides and eleven columns each along the long sides (counting the corner columns twice), enveloping the massive core wall of the *pronaos* and *cella*.

In early Christian times the temple was converted into a church. Dating from that time still is an improvised altar: on top of an ancient column stump lies an ancient capital, and on top of the capital an ancient stone slab. In order to Christianise these pagan parts of the building, the Greek letters IC XC were chiselled into the capital, standing for the name of Jesus Christ and still quite legible. Towards the south, east and west the uppermost terrace is surrounded by Doric colonnades from the first half of the 2nd century BC with 73 columns, replacing an even older structure that was completely made of wood. These *incubation halls* would be used by pilgrims looking for healing, for what was called 'healing sleep'. They expected that the god Asklípios would announce the suitable therapy to them in their sleep. They told their priests and doctors their dreams, who would then deduce the therapy from those dreams. As the sick were thus able to believe the god himself had ordered the right treatment, in many cases healing may well have been speeded up by psychosomatic processes. *May–Oct daily 8am–8pm, Nov–April Tue–Sun 8.30am–3pm | admission 4 euros | no bus, instead mini train from central bus station, return ticket 5 euros*

EMBRÓS THÉRME ★ ●
(115 E4) (🛈 L3)

The thermal spa of Kos doesn't really bear comparison with Bath or some Continental thermal baths, consisting only of a simple pump house and a stone circle in the sea right on the beach, forming a basin of about 10 m in diameter. This is where the thermal water, with a temperature of up to 40 °C/104 °F from a source in the rock, mixes with the seawater. One university's medical analysis attests to the water healing properties in cases of childhood development problems, as well as for skin conditions and problems with blood vessels and the respiratory tract. The simple *tavern (Moderate)* right next to the thermal waters has two pretty terraces where you can get value-for-money fish, as the tavern runs its own boat. A few sun loungers and sunshades are for hire along the small nearby pebble beaches. The thermal baths are located below the tarmac road, shortly before it ends. While the very steep track leading down to it can take a car, it's best to leave the car on the allocated places on the tarmac road. This is also where you'll find the shelter for the town bus. *Freely accessible at any time, even at night | 8 mi outside Kos Town*

PSALÍDI (115 E2) (🛈 L2)

Starting right next to the eastern limits of Kos Town, this area of settlement consists mainly of large good-quality hotels and a string of tavernas. The beaches are fairly narrow and often pebbly. Psalídi, the island's northwestern point, holds the *Psalídi Wetland*. With its lake of brackish water, those wetlands are an important stopping-off point for numerous migrating birds between autumn and spring, amongst them flamingos and herons. A *visitor centre* offers information on the importance of this habitat, sporadically in the summer, more frequently in winter. *Variable opening times | tel. 22 42 02 13 40 | www.biotopos.gr*

The Embrós Thérme are credited with various healing powers

THE CENTRE

As recently as four decades ago, many Koans lived as farmers in the villages of the interior. Today, these places have lost their economic importance; the money is being made in the coastal resorts.

Once, Tigáki, Marmári and Mastichári were only the ports serving the mountain villages; today they are the fountains of their wealth. Only Kardámena on the southern coast had always been a village of fishers and farmers.

ANTIMÁCHIA

(112 C4) *(⌖ E–F 4)* **With a population of 2200, Antimáchia is the second-largest inland village on Kos. It is situated on** a high plain in the centre of the island, where the sailcloth-covered blades of over 100 windmills were still turning in the 1920s.

Today, whilst the place is not that spectacular, it is worth a visit for its folklore museum.

SIGHTSEEING

TRADITIONAL HOUSE ★ ●

Antimáchia's cultural association has converted an old farmhouse diagonally opposite the windmill into a kind of folklore museum. Here you can see the way a 14-strong Antimáchia family was living up into the 1950s. One of the three rooms in the main house was the stables, while an extension held a spinning wheel and

Photo: The ruined castle of Antimáchia

Mountains, beaches and more – lively resorts and quiet mountain villages are only divided by a few miles of green landscape

oven. A stone basin in the front courtyard served to store the water fetched from the village well. The blades of the photogenic windmill opposite hardly ever go around any more, and no visits are possible. *Museum: Mon–Sat 9am–5pm, Sun 11am–3pm | admission 1.50 euros*

BUSES

Connections with Kos Town Mon–Sat approx. 6 times a day, Sun approx. 3 times. Also from the stop on the bypass road 3 to 4 times a day to Kardámena and Kéfalos.

FOOD & DRINK

The village only has one pastry bakery along the main road, plus several coffee bars.

WHERE TO GO

ANTIMÁCHIA CASTLE ※ ●
(113 D4) *(Ø F4)*
The road leading to Antimáchia Castle crosses a rugged high plain, with the

Treasures from the sea sold by a souvenir vendor in Kardámena harbour

long line of crenellations on the island's most impressive fortification looming against the sky from afar. The road ends in front of the northern gate of the fortification, which also served as a place of refuge. It was begun by the Venetians in the 13th century and completed by the Knights of St John in the 14th century. Once you've walked through the outer gate, you are standing in front of a second gate, where the coat of arms of the Grand Master of the Order, Pierre d'Aubusson, and the year 1494 can still be made out. Of the inside buildings practically nothing remains except a few cisterns. Only two small churches stand amidst the rampant vegetation of the castle's interior. Finally, there are some nice views from the southern edge of the castle over the extensive fertile coastal plain of Kardámena and across to the volcanic neighbouring island of Níssiros. *Freely accessible at any time | access signposted from the main road east of Antimáchia.*

AIRPORT (112 C5) (*Ⓜ E 4–5*)

With Aegean winds mostly blowing from the north, planes usually start their approach to Kos island from the south, passing as they lose height the volcanic island of Níssiros on the right hand side. The island's airport, situated on the southwestern edge of Antimáchia, has the official three-letter code KGS and lies at an altitude of 400 ft. The runway is oriented from southeast to northwest (for people in the know, this is called 15/33) and is just under 1.5 mi long. Kos has no limits on night flights, which can bring some grief to holidaymakers based in Kardámena. Killing time waiting before and after checking in is more fun and a lot cheaper at the INSIDER TIP *airport tavern (Budget)* opposite the terminal than inside the airport building. Keep an eye though on possible queues forming in front of the entrance to the terminal.

KARDÁMENA

(113 E5) *(⊠ G5)* **The only village of the Koan southern coast (pop. 1800) has no sights as such, nor does the beach really warrant a special trip. Head for the pedestrianised zone along the shore promenade.** This is where many cafés and bars ensure a busy nightlife. Kardámena is a popular destination for British tourists. All eateries, bars and shops are completely geared up towards visitors from the United Kingdom. On a Sunday, many restaurants serve Yorkshire pudding and roast beef, while providing an all-day English Breakfast too. Some pubs offer evening bingo, and all travel agencies rent out safes for cash and valuables. The long if narrow sand-and-pebble beaches stretch east and west from the village for some 2.5 mi each way.

FOOD & DRINK

Most restaurants are located on the shore promenade and the intersecting streets heading inland. Don't expect gastronomic delights here.

AVLÍ ★

Run by younger locals with a lot of zest, this tavern in a house built in 1902 right on the village square is a bit off the beaten track and the commotion of the promenade. The flower-bedecked inner courtyard is an Aegean idyll, the kitchen showing what it can do in its variety of small dishes and vegetarian delicacies. The wine cellar stores about 70 different wines from all over the world. *Platía | daily from 5pm onwards | www.avlirestaurant.gr | Expensive*

ENTERTAINMENT

Most clubs and music bars are located along the alley running parallel to the shore promenade and cater predominantly to a younger British clientele. Two of the most famous clubs are the *Status Disco Club* and the *Music Pub Downtown by Tony*.

MARCO POLO HIGHLIGHTS

★ **Traditional House**
See how a peasant family lived 50 years ago → p. 52

★ **Avlí**
Culinary oasis with an excellent wine list and an idyllic interior courtyard → p. 55

★ **Tam Tam**
Child-friendly beach restaurant in the middle of the dunes → p. 60

★ **Tomb of Harmylos**
An archaeological treat in a thoroughly Greek ambience → p. 62

★ **Paliá Pigí (Old Waterspring)**
The tavern at one of the oldest fountains on the island serves delicious grill dishes → p. 63

★ **Old Pýli (Paléa Pýli)**
A ghost village in the forest, a Byzantine ruined castle with panoramic views and a cosy café → p. 63

★ **Lagoúdi**
This village is still off the beaten track today, having remained the most authentic of all the villages in the centre of the island → p. 69

LOW BUDGET

▶ Holidaymakers living in the beach resorts along the northern coast get their groceries cheapest in the large Constantínos supermarkets on the access roads to Marmári and Tigáki.

▶ For the cheapest crossing from Kos to Kálimnos, take the ferries leaving from Mastichári **(112 B2)** *(ᗑ E3)*.

WHERE TO STAY

THE AEGEAN VILLAGE

Architecturally pleasing hotel complex in the style of a Greek village, 1500 m west of Kardámena on a low hill near the beach. Large pool and indoor pool open between October and May. In-house disco, five floodlit tennis courts, animation and water sports centre on the beach. *328 rooms | tel. 22 42 09 14 01 | www. aegean-village.com | Expensive*

INSIDER TIP ▶ OLYMPIA MARE ●

A Koan rarity: this two-storey house with 16 spacious and well-appointed apartments stands right on the beach with no road in between. Hammocks are strung up between tamarisks, sun loungers await in the shade of the tree. Your young host Níkos loves looking after his guests, while his mother serves water with a touch of saffron with the strong coffee. *1 mi west of town | tel. 22 42 09 17 11 | www.olympiamare.com | Moderate*

INFORMATION

From private travel agencies, i.e. *Kardámena Travel | tel. 22 42 09 13 71*

BUSES & FERRIES

Scheduled buses from Kos Town Mon–Sat 9.10am–9pm 6 times a day, Sun 9.10am–5pm 3 times. From Kardámena to Kos Town Mon–Sat 7.50am–5.10pm 6 times a day, Sun 7.50am–4pm 4 times; journey time: 45 min. Buses to Paradise Beach and Kéfalos twice a day; town bus from the main square on the harbour approx. 9am–1am 11 times a day, to the Norída Beach hotel in the east and the Aegean Village hotel in the west. Day trip buses to Paradise Beach (return 7 euros) | FOOT PASSENGER ferries to the neighbouring island of Níssiros Mon–Sat approx. 2pm, pleasure boats daily approx. 9am. Also on offer are 90-minute sunset cruises (7 euros).

MARMÁRI

(113 E1) *(ᗅ G2)* **Before the tourists arrived, Marmári (pop. 460) was only the landing place for the fishermen of Pýli.** These days, Marmári has turned into a cluster of smaller and larger hotels, which however keep a good distance from each other. They all enjoy the use of the village's miles of wide sandy beach. In the centre and in front of the larger hotels the beach has sun loungers and sunshades; other sections lie as empty as they always did in front of a belt of low dunes. Between June and November you're bound to see grazing cows. They are allowed to feed on what's left on the fields after the grain harvest, and like taking the odd trip to the beach.

FOOD & DRINK

APOSTÓLIS

Grill tavern with a shady terrace under palm trees; rural atmosphere, friendly service. The hosts serve fresh produce from their large garden. *Main street, about 500 m from the beach | daily | Budget*

TWINS

Your host Olimbía's speciality is rabbit *stifádo*, i.e. rabbit with onion vegetables in a red sauce. *On a crossroads of the road to Tigáki | daily | Budget*

ENTERTAINMENT

Marmári is not exactly Clubbing Central. Holidaymakers here prefer to sit in airy garden bars listening to some good mu-

Holiday atmosphere along the miles of beach at Marmári

sic, and maybe have the occasional late-night boogie.

IMAGES CLUB
Garden bar, which up to 11pm functions as a music café and then as a club. *On the road leading off the coast road, 120 m from the sea | daily from 7pm*

INSIDER TIP ▶ DANCING INSEL
It's hard not to get talking to other guests at the long counter of this garden bar, run by a windsurfing instructor and his team. *On the road leading off the coast road, about 500 m from the sea | daily from 6pm*

WHERE TO STAY

CARAVIA BEACH
Consisting of a five-storey main building and a string of bungalows, this large hotel right on the sandy beach is particularly suitable for active holidaymakers. There are various water sports on offer, but also table tennis, mini golf or tennis. The hotel also has a freshwater pool and its own bike rental. *298 rooms | about 1000 m east of Marmári | tel. 22 42 04 12 91 | www.caraviabeach.com | Expensive*

INSIDER TIP ▶ CAVO D'ORO
Quiet apartment complex right on the beach, with restaurant, beach bar and garden, particularly good for families. About 400 m east of the village centre. *21 apartments | tel. 22 42 04 18 00 | www.cavodorohotel.gr | Moderate*

MARMÁRI BEACH
Large, yet architecturally pleasing hotel with villa-type individual buildings in an extensive garden complex in a rural setting. The sandy beach is only about 150 m away; guests also have the use of three large freshwater pools. Between July and September, children can be looked after in the Mini Club. There is a large range of activities on offer for guests: volleyball, beach ball, crazy golf and tryout lessons in tennis, windsurfing and catamaran sailing are free of charge. For a charge, the hotel offers courses in tennis, mountain biking, windsurfing, catamaran sailing, archery and inline skating. *320 rooms sleeping 2–4 people (only bookable on an all-inclusive basis) | tel. 22 42 04 12 19 | Expensive*

INFORMATION

Information is only available from the private travel agencies in the village.

BUSES

Bus connections with Kos Town Mon–Sat approx. 12 times a day, Sun approx. 7 times, journey time approx. 35 min.

KOMBOLÓI

Older Greek men in particular always carry a kombolói, constantly letting it glide through their fingers. The little chain resembles a rosary, but has no religious significance, rather serving just to pass the time. The Greeks probably developed it as a variation on the Islamic prayer chain. A kombolói may be bought at any kiosk, or indeed in fancy versions in silver or amber from jewellers.

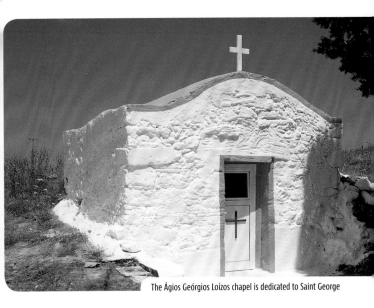

The Ágios Geórgios Loízos chapel is dedicated to Saint George

MASTICHÁRI

(112 B–C2) (*E3*) **Amongst the three holiday spots on the northern coast, Mastichári (pop. 370) has best managed to hold on to some of its village character.**

Most houses have one or two storeys only, lending the village a quiet and intimate rather than a loud and busy atmosphere. Another bonus for Mastichári is the harbour, which is used by day tripper boats and a car ferry.

SIGHTSEEING

ÁGIOS IOÁNNIS BASILICA

The remains of an Early Christian basilica from around AD 500 stand on a low rise on the beach. The layout of the church is still clearly visible. In the northeastern corner, you can see the font set into the floor of the former baptismal chapel. The early Christians were baptised by full immersion, as is still the case in the Orthodox Church today. To find the basilica, head east from the large euros Village hotel on the western end of the shore promenade, beyond the small dry bed of a brook.

ÁGIOS GEÓRGIOS LOÍZOS CHURCH

The small white chapel dedicated to Saint George was erected in medieval times using stone blocks and column stumps from ancient buildings. *Freely accessible at any time | coming from Kos Town, the church is standing on the right hand side of the road, just over a mile after leaving the main road in the direction of Mastichári*

SCULPTURE PARK ●

On the grounds of one of the island's foremost hotels, the Bavarian sculptor

Peter R Müller was allowed to recreate the world of ancient gods and myths from iron and scrap metal. Here, Zeus is throwing neon-coloured lightning, Prometheus is bringing fire to humans, and Poseidon is guiding his rusty steeds. *Neptune Resort | between Mastichári and Marmári | sculpture park freely accessible*

FOOD & DRINK

KALÍ KARDIÁ

At its inauguration in 1955, the 'Good Heart' was the only restaurant far and wide. The old hospitality is still there, while the range of food has been adapted to holidaymakers' needs. An entire dentex (dog's teeth) fish with boiled potatoes and fresh vegetables is charged at a fixed price, rather than by weight, as is often the case in other places. Early birds come like to come here for a morning coffee: the place is the only one to open at 7am. *On the harbour across from the bus stop | daily | Budget*

KÁLYMNOS

This restaurant's very friendly host Periklís rejects gastronomic globalisation. You order fish, you get fish – and no fries with that. Side dishes are ordered separately. Calamari can be had cheaply from the deep freezer, or a bit more expensive fresh from the Aegean Sea. One of the special specialities, as it were, are the tiny prawns from the island of Sêmi, which sadly don't always feature on the menu. If they do, make sure you go for them. *On the harbour | daily | Expensive*

TAM TAM ★ ●

This garden tavern is located on a dune right on the broad sandy beach; cows graze on the pastures beyond. Children find plenty of space for games, adults up for a chat an inviting bar counter, and

shopaholics a shop with breezy beachwear reminiscent of the hippie era. The choice of dishes ranges from pizza to fresh fish. *2 mi east of Mastichári | daily | Moderate*

INSIDER TIP TRADITIONAL GREEK HOUSE ☺

Terrace walls built from natural stone, one corner furnished like a traditional farmhouse room and a stone oven still used for producing home-made bread are the hallmarks of this restaurant on the western beach of Mastichári. Your host Sávvas is originally from Kéfalos, his wife Ioánna from Antimáchia. They take great care to only source chickens, meat, cheese and many other ingredients from their relations, enabling them to guarantee freshness and quality. Portions are large, service more on the rustic and hearty side than perfect, and a lot of good olive oil is used in the cooking. If you don't like it quite so oily, just say 'me polí lígo ládi, parakaló', with very little oil! *Access from the beach west of the harbour, or from the one-way road leading out of the village (look for a small signpost) | daily | Budget*

SHOPPING

INSIDER TIP PIA & IRA ☺

While the two women owners don't produce any of the jewellery and souvenirs for sale, they have excellent taste. Both are also active in animal welfare, can receive feed donations and are always looking for foreign adoptive parents for young dogs. *On the main pedestrian street*

BEACHES & SWIMMING

Along the miles of sandy beach starting immediately west and east of Mastichári harbour, you can find sections with shade-giving tamarisks. Even a little east from the harbour there is a short section of beach in front of some low cliffs. Between Mastichári and Marmári dunes run along the broad band of sand; many sections of the beach here are free of sunshades and sun loungers.

LIDO WATER PARK

On a 20-acres site this large aqua park opposite the land-facing side of the large hotels east of Mastichári offers all sorts of water slides, a wave pool, whirlpools, a Lazy River and a pool for playing waterball. *On the road running close to the beach in the direction of Marmári | daily 10am–7pm | www.lidowaterpark.com | Admission approx. 20 euros*

ENTERTAINMENT

HAMLET

Having worked as a bar manager on luxury liners, your host Pávlos Zoís is rightly considered one of the most professional cocktail mixers on the island. His café bar doesn't owe its name to William Shakespeare's Danish prince, but rather to the English word for a small village. *East of the water park on the road leading to the beach*

INSIDER TIP▶ NUMBER ONE BAR

Bar with terrace under vines, often with dancing. *Daily from 8pm | between the one-way street leading out of the village and the western beach*

WHERE TO STAY

NEPTUNE RESORT

Themed gardens and a sculpture park are an early indication that this hotel likes to be different. Alongside rooms and suites there are apartments sleeping up to five; the spa area has a classically elegant design. A spacious pool zone, a broad range of water sports on offer and

The way to the Neptune Resort leads you past a sculpture garden

a mountainbike station offering guided tours as well all form part of the high-class amenities and special character of this beach resort. *On the Mastichári-Marmári road | tel. 22 42 04 14 80 | www. neptune.gr | Expensive*

INSIDER TIP PHILIPPOS

Small apartment house with a very friendly owner, at the entrance to Mas-tichári village, some 600 m from the beach. *Eight studios sleeping up to three people | tel. 22 42 05 14 55 | Budget*

SEA BREEZE

Kóstas and Eléni Diakanastássi, who speak good English, create a family atmosphere in their small hotel on the harbour. Some of the rooms and apart-ments have a balcony with sea view. *20 rooms | 100 m to the right of the junction of the access road and the coastal road | tel. 22 42 05 91 73 | www.seabreezekos. gr | Budget*

BUSES & FERRIES

A bus runs three to five times a day be-tween Mastichári and Kos. Journey time: roughly 45 mins. Car ferries connect Mastichári at least three times a day with Póthia, the capital of the neighbouring island of Kálimnos. There is also a small fast passenger ferry running several times a day; its timetable is synchronised to fit the arrivals and departures of the scheduled flight to and from Athens. *Timetables from www.anemferries.gr and www.kalymna-yachting.gr*

PÝLI

(113 E2–3) *(ฟ G3)* **With 2400 inhabit-ants, Pýli is the largest village in the centre of the island.**

The village is spread across the lower part of the village, Ágios Geórgios, and the prettier upper part, Ágios Nikólaos. There are no official accommodation providers in Pýli.

SIGHTSEEING

INSIDER TIP VILLAGE FOUNTAIN

A testimony to the watery wealth of this part of the island is the pretty fountain that was built from stone blocks and received its current appearance in 1592. Day and night the precious liquid bub-bles out of gargoyles, some of which have the shape of a lion's head. *Freely ac-cessible | 150 m west of the village square*

TOMB OF HARMYLOS ★

A nearly hidden signpost on a pylon in a sharp right-hand bend on the tarmac road leading to Kardámena points the way to an unusual tomb. Legend attributes the vaulted tomb chamber with six niches on its two longer sides to the ancient hero Harmylos, the mythical founding father of the first Koan ruling dynasty. This is where he was honoured, together with the twelve Olympic gods. Standing above the tomb was a small Ionian colonnade, of which only a few fragments remain, scattered on the floor. The hall's back wall was later reused as a lateral wall for the small chapel dedicated to Christ. On the western side two beautiful ancient blocks with a relief frieze, an inscription stone and an Early Christian cross relief were inserted into the chapel wall.

You'll often see two elderly ladies from the nearby farmhouse sitting outside the chapel to explain the saints represented on the icons to visitors of the church, and make them a present of sweets and blossoms or aromatic herbs afterwards. *About 5 mins. from the village square | freely accessible during the daytime*

EVANGELISMÓS CHURCH

The paintings inside this small chapel were started in 1987. The first fresco to be completed was a representation of the Annunciation, which the church is dedicated to, on the right-hand lateral wall. We see the archangel approaching Mary to bring her the good news. *On the village square | open during the daytime*

FOOD & DRINK

PALIÁ PIGÍ (OLD WATERSPRING) ★

In this small tavern by the village fountain, Geórgios and Evangelía spoil their guests below a shady *ficus benjamina* tree with delicious fried aubergine and courgette slices, small *soúvlaki* skewers and *sousoukákia* mincemeat sausages from the charcoal grill. *Daily | Budget*

SHOPPING

INSIDER TIP ▶ BUS STOP GALLERY

Kurt Hlavacek, aka ● 'Sol', exhibits his paintings here. His Dutch wife Nel Bezemer sells jewellery, artworks and crafts made by their Greek friends. If you're interested to take up painting, or improve your skills, the artist can arrange individual tuition. *80 m below the Platía on the main street | in summer daily 9am–9pm| www.busstopgallery.kosweb.com*

REMKO AND RIA

The artist couple Remko de Gilde and Ria Hessels have been living in Pýli since 1978. Remko's watercolours and etchings capture the enchantment of the Koan landscape, while Ria manufactures original silver jewellery, some set with semi-precious stones. *On the village square*

BUSES

Bus connections with Kos Town Mon–Sat

Village fountain in Pýli

approx. 5 times a day, Sun 3 times, journey time 30 minutes

WHERE TO GO

OLD PÝLI (PALÉA PÝLI) ★
(113 F3) (*Ø H3*)

The most romantic ruins on Kos occupy a lonely position on the northern slope of the island's mountain range on a steep rock: the scattered remains of a village inhabited since medieval times and only abandoned in 1830 after a cholera epidemic. The village was not visible from the sea and so was well protected from pirate attacks. The houses have tumbled down now, but four of the medieval churches are still standing. Two of them are particularly atmospheric: on the lower edge of the village, the *Asómati Taxiárches Gavriíl ke Michaíl* church dedicated to the bodiless archangels, with sparse fresco fragments, and on a small plateau below the castle the large *Panagía ton Kastrianón* dedicated to the Virgin Mary. The latter was built as early as the 11th century and holds fresco fragments from the 14th century. The chairs you see stacked inside all year round are

needed once a year for the big church feast on the first two days of February for pilgrims who come together for a merry meal. The 11th-century 🌿 *ruined Byzantine castle* on the summit of the rock offers magnificent panoramic views across the island's northern coast.

The tarmac road on the castle hill turns into a track that is only navigable by jeep. A few paces on, a sign to the left indicates the path leading up the slope to 🌿 *Café Ória* where Geórgios and Michális have created a particularly cosy café right in front of the house they were born in. At practically the same altitude as the castle, the café offers splendid views. Between about the end of May and the end of September, your hosts offer a special service: **INSIDER TIP** mules waiting at the

The location of the ruined castle of Old Pýli guarantees good views

start of the path to take guests up to the café. *Open during the daytime | Budget*

TIGÁKI

(114 A2) (*💷 H2*) With its miles of narrow sandy beach, Tigáki (pop. 230) is the closest beach resort to Kos Town on the island's northern coast. The centre is marked by a roundabout with a few taverns and snack bars clustering around it. The beach has no shade-giving trees or dunes further back. The hotels are set at a distance from each other, with goats, sheep and ● cows grazing between them, as they do in the two other villages along the northern coast.

SIGHTSEEING

ALÍKI SALT PANS

The former salt pans, where no salt has been harvested for a long time, today enjoys environmental protection. In the winter months, numerous water birds make their home here, amongst them flamingos. *Freely accessible | 800 m west of the roundabout*

FOOD & DRINK

INSIDER TIP ▶ AMBÉLI 😊

The walls of this idyllic garden tavern are decorated with Greek sayings, plaits of garlic and decorative pumpkins. The hosts serve many vegetarian specialities made from fresh vegetables, but also rustic dishes such as *piktí*, a Koan variation on pig jelly. *Off the shore road, about 1.5 mi east of the roundabout (watch out for the signpost there) | daily | Moderate*

PLÓRI

Your host Michális and his son Jánnis prefer to serve fish, with the cheaper farmed options pointed out on the menu. Side dishes and salads are ordered separately. Particular treats are fish in salt crust and sole in garlic butter. Every day, the dessert selection will include a home-made, relatively low-sugar variety. *On the shore road 80 m west of the roundabout | daily | Expensive*

WHERE TO STAY

TIGÁKI BEACH

No great shakes architecturally, but a comfortable hotel for a beach holiday, only about 100 m from the beach and about 300 m from the roundabout. Pretty, slightly old-fashioned garden with palm trees, araucarias and banana trees, as well as a freshwater pool. *169 rooms | east of the roundabout | tel. 22 42 06 94 46 | www.tigakibeach-kos. com | Moderate–Expensive*

INFORMATION

Only from private travel agencies, e. g. *Tigáki Express | tel. 22 42 06 90 00*

BUSES

Bus connection with Kos Town Mon–Sat approx. 12 times, Sun approx. 7 times, journey time 15 minutes

WHERE TO GO

ÁGIOS PÁVLOS BASILICA
(114 A3) (ഗ H2)

The remains of a basilica dedicated to the St Paul on the edge of Tigáki occupy an idyllic position in the middle of a green landscape. All that is preserved here are the high walls of the baptismal chapel, with a cruciform baptismal font and a few foundation walls. The floor mosaics discovered here have been covered with gravel, for their own protection, and cannot be viewed unfortunately. *Freely accessible | coming from Tigáki past the sign marking the end of Zipári behind the bridge immediately right of the main road*

ÁGIOS IOÁNNIS CHURCH
(114 B2–3) (ഗ H2)

Coming from Tigáki, 750 m past the sign marking the end of Zipari village, follow a blue signpost pointing you to 'Saint John'. The small chapel was erected immediately above a tiny cave church, where remains of the altar and some murals can still be made out. The modern chapel above has numerous icons representing John the Baptist in many different ways. *Freely accessible*

ZIPÁRI (114 A3) (ഗ H2)

In the large one-street village of Zipári, a signpost points to the Early Christian ruins of the *Capáma Basilica* on the edge of the upper part of the village. What you can see here is a well-preserved apse and a cruciform baptismal basin.

ZÍA

(114 A4) (ഗ H3) **Once, Zía was the island's picture-book village, owing its wealth to its water resources.**

Today, Zía makes its living from tourism first and foremost: some days, you can see a dozen tour buses on the small village square at the lower edge of town. In administrative terms, Zía belongs to the Asfendíou municipality, which also includes Lagoúdi and Evangelistría.

SIGHTSEEING

KÍMISSIS TIS THEOTÓKOU CHURCH

What you see today of the church in the upper part of the village dates from 1919. Its entire interior was painted between 1992 and 1995 with frescoes in the traditional Byzantine style. Only the entrance area (narthex) has so far not received a new coat of paint. On the left-hand northern wall, the first part of the image shows the Greeks' surprisingly informal approach to their saints: the chest of the Archangel Michael bears the fuse box for the church lighting. A donor's inscription above the northern door honours Geórgios Katimetzóglou, who painted the frescoes. The most impressive amongst them are the representations of several events from the New Testament. On the northern part of the wall, on the left-hand side, you can make out, amongst other things, Christ's descent into the Hades river:

having broken down the gates of Hell he is now freeing Adam and Eva, standing behind him, as well as the two kings David and Solomon, the first to be liberated from the netherworld. On the southern part of the wall, to the right, you can see the Dormition – literally, the 'Falling Asleep' – of Mary: Jesus and the Apostles are standing at the deathbed of the Virgin Mary, and Jesus has already taken her soul, represented as a swaddled child, into his hands, to take it to heaven. *Open all day*

FOOD & DRINK

AVLÍ
Classic tavern appreciated by its Greek guests for its fine grilled meats. Particularly popular is *pantsétta*, charcoal-grilled pork belly. *On the main street | daily | Moderate*

SMARAGD
Tavern with excellent panoramic and sunset views from the ☼ roof terrace; good food, very friendly hosts. *20 m above the village church | daily | Budget*

INSIDER TIP ▶ SUNSET BALCONY ☼
This aptly named tavern is indeed the best place in the village to experience this natural spectacle. Your hosts Sérgos and his wife Chrissoúla serve delicious sundowner *souvláki*, fried courgette and aubergine slices or *revithókeftédes*, a kind of pancake make from chickpea flour. *On the small alley leading from the square to the church | daily | Budget*

SHOPPING

If you're after authentic souvenirs, this is not the place to come to, as nothing is produced in Zía any more. All the wares on offer come from elsewhere in Greece,

View from Zía onto the church of Lagoúdi and the wide plain

if not from further afield even. Cinnamon and saffron don't grow in the Mediterranean. Not that this seems to make a great dent in turnover here.

ENTERTAINMENT

FANTASÍA

While the village settles down to rest after the sun has gone down, hundreds of holidaymakers sit a bit below, on the main road to Kos Town, in this large open-air tavern, watching Greek folk dances, even joining in a bit later on. Food is a set menu, and the wine policy is 'drink-as-much-as-you-like' – and can handle. In the brochures promoting this 'Greek evening', the restaurant is compared to an amphitheatre for its location on a slope – a bit of an exaggeration. Whether you visit or not is up to you: if you come for the show only, you'll be properly entertained and might well enjoy it. And at least Vasílis Trákas, the tavern owner, is a local boy – born and bred in the hamlet of Lagoúdi – rather than a big shot from Athens. *Daily 8pm–midnight | tel. 22 42 06 95 15 | Expensive*

The souvenir shops in Zía sell everything you never needed

BUSES

Bus connections with Kos Town Mon–Sat 4 times a day, no buses running on Sun, journey time about 40 minutes

WHERE TO GO

DÍKEOS MOUNTAIN
(114 B4) *(⌖ H–J3)*

Zía is the base for climbing Díkeos (2765 ft), the island's highest mountain. Depending on fitness levels, hikers need between three and five hours to go up and back down. The footpath starts at the small cobbled square in the upper part of the village, where you'll usually see some cars parked. From here, steps leading uphill join a track, from which more steps lead to an unpaved road that you follow uphill to the right. At the next fork in the road, marked by a bell hanging in a tree belonging to the *Isódia tis Theotókou* chapel, keep right. After a few minutes a track forks off uphill to the left, marked by a signpost with a white cross on a red background. From here, all the remaining path to the summit is marked by red dots. Just before reaching the highest point on Díkeos, the *Metamórfosis tou Christoú* chapel announces the presence of a monastery that has been here since the late 11th century.

Minimum requirements for the hike to the summit of Díkeos are shoes with good grip, something to cover the head, and water. If you can, start the tour in the early morning, so you are already descending when the midday heat hits.

EVANGELÍSTRIA (114 A4) *(⌖ H3)*

The main square of this hamlet, with its *Evangelismós tis Theotókou* church (1910) visible from afar, lies right on the main road from Zía to Zipári and Kos Town (bus stop). Since 1987, the inside of the church is gradually being painted in frescoes in traditional Byzantine style. *Open all day in the daytime*

LAGOÚDI ★ (114 A4) *(⌖ H3)*

This small hamlet with some 120 inhabitants is located just 500 m off the main road from Zía to Kos Town, yet has been spared most of the onslaught of mass tourism. Cockerels are free to roam on the village street, and in the village's kafeníon time seems to have stood still. The centre of the village is marked by the slightly elevated ● *Panagía Theotókou Genesíou* church dedicated to the birth of the Virgin Mary. The murals inside date mostly from between 1985 and 1997. Often village priest Kyriákos or his sister drop into the church; both enjoy meeting visitors. *Daily 11am–6pm*

Next to the street leading up to the church, a track leads down and after only 20 m passes the fascinating INSIDERTIP▶ *Beautiful Greece / I Oréa Elláda estate*. A Flemish lady, Christina Zentéli-Colman, who has lived here for decades, has turned the place into a paradise for lovers of antiques, painting and jewellery, and good food and drink. Two holiday apartments give that truly rural holiday feeling. Christina serves a daily changing main dish and excellent wines on the terrace of the café, exhibiting her paintings inside, and the antiques she has collected on the island in the rooms looking on to the garden. These antiques are for sale, as are the antique jewellery. The two holiday flats in the old house, built from stone, share a terrace and have quirky furniture. *Café and shops daily 10am–10pm | tel. 22 42 06 90 04, mobile tel. 69 73 49 20 31*

THE WEST

West of Antimáchia Kos changes its face. Until you reach Kéfalos, the often straight-as-a-die road passes not a single village. Sporadically single houses stand by the roadside.

Most of the soil is barren, with only juniper thriving here. In the spring, when herbs and rockroses are in bloom, the whole area is enveloped in an aromatic fragrance. In summer this is replaced by a rather more steppe-type feeling, reinforced by the near-uninhabited Kéfalos peninsula looming to the west. While only minutes away, the wealth of this area can't be appreciated from the roadside: a multitude of superb sandy beaches that have seen few tourists.

The fairly gentle coast in the north and the steeper coast in the south are fringed by a long belt of sand. Small tracks lead via steep bends to the beaches of the southern coast. For the most part these beaches are still completely unspoilt and devoid of people. There is no planning permission for any hotels or guesthouses here. Only out to the east one Robinson Club has been established. The beach on the northern coast may not even be cleaned, so that a lot of flotsam and jetsam is lying around. Which explains that the area attracts only a few swimmers and a handful of kitesurfers. Even the *Caretta caretta* marine turtle, threatened with extinction, can lay her eggs here in peace and quiet.

At the western end of the southern coast lies the small port of *Kamári*. In summer this section of the coast is used as an ad-

Photo: Remains of the Early Christian basilica of Ágios Stéfanos

The other side of Kos – in the rural west you'll find untouched nature and dream beaches with few visitors

ditional mooring place by pleasure boats arriving at the temporary jetty of *Skála*. A little bit east of there, the columns of the Early Christian basilica of *Ágios Stéfanos* stick out of the sand opposite the uninhabited rocky islet of *Kastrí*. Behind the beach, between Skála and the basilica, archaeologists have found the remnants of an ancient port settlement in the sand.

KÉFALOS

(110 C3) *(∅ B6)* **Of all the settlements on the island, this large interior village has best managed to hold on to its traditional character.**

Lying on the edge of the hilly Kéfalos peninsula, where Kos' natural heritage has not been altered by houses and hotels, Kéfalos was the first capital of the island, called *Astypalaia* at the time. It was abandoned only when an earth-

Mosaics from the Ágios Stéfanos basilica

them upright – most however have since fallen over again. The layout of the basilica can still be made out. Leaning on the northern wall stood a second, smaller church with a cruciform baptismal font on the floor that is still very well preserved. Floor mosaics found here were covered up again with gravel. *Admission free at any time | on the beach immediately west from the former Club Méditerranée; access from the main road via the narrow road beginning immediately to the right of the Club's barrier*

RUINED CASTLE

In the same way as many other places, the medieval village of Kéfalos was once secured by a castle. Of this castle only a few ruined walls are left, from which the view ranges across the coastal plain below. *Admission free at any time | on reaching the mountain village, turn off to the right onto the car park and drive on the road crossing it for another 50 m*

KASTRÍ ISLAND

The tiny rocky island just offshore from the Kámbos plain beach and the Ágios Stéfanos basilica is uninhabited. All there is to see is a small and usually locked church dedicated to Saint Anthony. It is possible to INSIDER TIP reach the islet half-swimming, half wading between buoys which are there to stop motorboats and windsurfers from passing.

ISÓDIA TIS PANAGÍAS CHURCH

The town's main church is dedicated to the Entry into The Temple of the Most Holy Mother of God. It was funded in 1873 by a high-ranking official from Egypt, which like Kos was once part of the Ottoman Empire. Inside, the church is completely covered in murals in the traditional Byzantine style.

quake destroyed the town in 412 BC and the inhabitants left to found Kos Town in the farthest east of the island.

SIGHTSEEING

ÁGIOS STÉFANOS BASILICA ★

If you appreciate unusual places to swim, you will love this opportunity for a dip at the most beautiful Early Christian basilica of the island. If you like, catch the sun between columns and walls that are 1500 years old, and only ten steps away from the water. The relatively well-preserved walls stand on a slight elevation right above the beach of the Kámbos plain, and diagonally across from the rocky islet of *Kastrí*. Italian archaeologists have restored a few of the columns and placed

FOOD & DRINK

INSIDER TIP KATERINA ☺

This simple tavern on the eastern end of the Ágios Stéfanos beach has an ideal location for a dip followed by a food-stop. The owner's family bake their own bread and serve eggs laid by their own hens. Every day, the owner picks up fresh fish from the harbour. *Daily | Budget*

INSIDER TIP MEGÁLO MÝLOS ⌖

This cosy café working out of a newly constructed windmill with indoor and outdoor seating boasts a spectacular location with panoramic views. The coffee tastes just as good as the cake. *Outside Kéfalos on the road to Limniónas | daily | Moderate*

STAMATÍA

One of the oldest restaurants on Kámbos Beach. Once all you could find were fish dishes and soúvlaki skewers; today, the kitchen has adapted to the wishes of the tourists, preparing soups and vegetarian dishes too. Another concession is that the fresh fish is also offered in portions, at a fixed price. In the winter, owner Antónis is busy looking after his olive trees, which is why the kitchen uses only oil from their own production. *Skála, immediately east of the jetty | daily | Expensive*

SHOPPING

Neither Kéfalos nor Kámbos have large supermarkets or souvenir shops, but you can get groceries and items of daily use from several small shops in either place.

BEACHES

In the western part of Kámbos town, the beach is only a few metres wide, running immediately below the road. From the jetty in *Skála* onwards the beach becomes wider again, and prettier, too, with the most beautiful part of the sandy beach between the *Ágios Stéfanos Basilica* and the eastern end of the bay at the Katerína tavern. From the nearby beaches around the area, *Paradise Beach* can be reached directly by bus or by sea taxi from Skála.

★ **Ágios Stéfanos basilica**
A beach for those with a sense of history? That too is an option on Kos; soak up the sun right next to the basilica ruins → p. 72

★ **Pántheon**
This remote apartment hotel high above the plain of Kámbos scores with silence and fabulous views → p. 74

★ **Ágios Ioánnis Theológos**
Empty little sandy beaches, a tavern and a windsurfing zone with strong swell, for the pros → p. 75

★ **Ágios Ioánnis Pródromos monastery**
The former monastery with sweeping views over an unspoilt landscape is a popular picnic spot → p. 76

★ **Magic Beach**
A usually empty section of the longest island beach, where you can make like Adam and Eve and discard your clothes to lie in the sun → p. 78

★ **Paradise Beach (Bubble Beach)**
The liveliest section of the longest island beach, with a taverna and a lot of water sports → p. 78

MARCO POLO HIGHLIGHTS

KÉFALOS

ENTERTAINMENT

B 52
This cocktail bar boasts a pretty terrace, which often serves as a lively dance floor after midnight, when the doors are closed. *On the coastal road between Skála and Kamári next to the small Hotel Sydney*

POPEYE'S BAR
With its music policy revolving around vintage tracks, this club tends to attract a clientele over 30. *On the main road on the coastal plain | daily from 5pm*

SIWA CLUB
This disco for a younger crowd in the west of the island sometimes has live music on too. *On the main road on the coastal plain, 100 m east of Popeye's Bar*

INSIDER TIP SURVIVOR
A club that lives up to its name, opening only at midnight. *Kámbos, on the main road towards the airport*

WHERE TO STAY

HERMES
Romantic spirits choosing this hotel on a slope between the Kámbos plain and the mountain village of Kéfalos will enjoy the ☀ pool terrace with a view over the entire bay and a music bar with dancing. Owners Sebastian and Diana have perfect English, with the British making up the majority of their guests. *50 rooms | on the main road from Kámbos to Kéfalos | tel. 22 42 07 11 02 | www.kefalos.com/hermes | Moderate*

INSIDER TIP KAMÁRI BAY
Friendly hotel with a family atmosphere, some 200 m from the beach. Having lived in New York for 35 years, owner Jánnis Manolákis speaks perfect English; many of his guests are from the UK. Pool with splash pool, very good value for money. *40 rooms | in the Skála part of town near the island's main road| tel. 22 42 07 15 56 | Budget*

PANORAMA STUDIOS ☀
Set high above the eastern end of Ágios Stéfanos Bay, this house with 17 apartments sleeping two to four people boasts a magnificent view while only 15 minutes on foot from the beach. Here, most guests are German, which explains the breakfast cheese, made from the milk of the owners' goats. Your breakfast egg will have been laid that very day probably. The nearest bus stop is a two-minute walk away. *tel. 22 42 07 15 24 | www.panorama-kefalos.gr | Moderate*

PÁNTHEON ★ ☀
From its remote position high above the Kámbos plain, this apartment hotel boasts a fabulous view, whilst only about 1000 m from the beach. Manager Bábis himself drives his guests in a shuttle bus five times down to Skála (starting at 10am) and back (up to 11.30pm). All 25 studios have a balcony with sea view; a small bar serves as a cosy meeting point. *On the road branching off right towards Kéfalos from the main road sloping down into the Kámbos plain, at the Panórama guesthouse | tel. 22 42 07 19 00, in winter tel. 22 42 07 12 37 | Budget*

INFORMATION
General tourist enquiries can be addressed to private travel agencies, i.e. *Kástri Holidays | tel. 22 42 07 17 55 | www.kefalos.com*

BUSES
Bus connection with Kos Town Mon–Sat

The tavern at Ágios Ioánnis Theológos is the only one for miles

4 to 6 times a day, Sun 3 times. If you want to go to Kardámena, change in Antimáchia

In the summer season, a ferry runs to the neighbouring island of Níssiros up to five times a week

ÁGIOS IOÁNNIS THEOLÓGOS ★ ●
(110 A4) (∅ A7)

Few visitors find the way to these near-unspoilt sandy beaches that line the juniper-covered dunes, and few sun loungers are available. Often a strong swell attracts windsurfers who enjoy braving the strong winds with their own board. The one beach tavern serves excellent Greek food. The small chapel at the end of the gravel track leading to the beach is dedicated to John the Evangelist. The key hangs above the door and can just be picked up there – probably because the interior of the church is nearly bare. The chapel is reached on a good track signposted from the main road towards the Ágios Ioánnis Pródromos monastery 2.5 miles away. 4.5 miles from Kéfalos

ANCIENT THEATRE (ARCHÉO THÉATRO/ PALÁTIA) ☀ ● (110 C4) (∅ B6)

The paltry remains of the theatre of the ancient town of Astypalaia lie amidst a fragrant pine forest on the edge of a deep gorge. The only thing to see now are the remnants of two rows of seats and a few fragments of the stage building from the 2nd century BC, i.e. Hellenistic times. 10 m left from the exit you can spot very sparse remains of an ancient Demeter sanctuary. The theatre is located a mile past the end of the mountain village of Kéfalos. To the left of the tarmac road leading to the Ágios Ioánnis Pródromos monastery, the way to the theatre complex leads after about 30 m through an (always open) gate in the wire fence.

CAMEL BEACH (111 D2) (🗺 C6)

A steep unmade road leads down to this small remote bay between the two mile-long beaches at Kéfalos. The beach is only about 100 m long; climbing over rocks will lead you to other tiny sandy spots, where nudist bathing is an option. Of all the beaches around Kéfalos this is the most attractive for snorkellers. A simple taverna provides food and drink. The access is signposted from the main road, 600 m away.

CAVO PARADISO BEACH (110 B6) (🗺 B8)

Few visitors find their way to this ensemble of three small sandy coves in the *Ormós Chilandríou* bay below Cape Kriélos, rising up a steep 879 feet from the sea. The best way to get to Cavo Paradiso is on a track (a bit rough in parts) starting at Theológos Beach and running close to the coast. *8.5 mi from Kéfalos*

KÁTI (110 A4) (🗺 A7)

Completely without shade and attracting few visitors, this beach on the western coast, 300 metres long, is reached via a rough track. *4.5 mi from Kéfalos*

PANAGÍA I PALATIANÍ CHURCH 🌿 (110 C3) (🗺 B6–7)

The small chapel, only built in 1988 and given whitewashed walls and a blue vaulted ceiling, can be seen for miles, without having much architectural interest. However, only 15 m away, a ruined chapel dedicated to the Virgin Mary was erected using carefully worked blocks of an ancient temple which used to stand here. *Modern chapel always locked, the ruins freely accessible | 1000 m behind the end of the mountain village of Kéfalos, 200 m off the tarmac road leading to the Ágios Ioánnis Pródromos monastery*

ÁGIOS IOÁNNIS PRÓDROMOS MONASTERY ★ 🌿 (110 B5) (🗺 B7)

Also called *Ágios Ioánnis Thymianós*, the small former monastery today stands alone and lost above the western coast of Kos. From the end of the access road, 43 steps lead down to the monastery terrace, where an ancient plane tree in

'KOZ' OR 'KOSS'?

Many foreigners end up asking themselves right up to the last day of their holiday how the name of island and town should be pronounced exactly. The answer is clear. For one, the contemporary Greek language possesses no closed long vowels. Secondly, the Greek letter sigma – i.e. 's' – is always pronounced as a sibilant and voiceless. Thus Kos is pronounced 'Koss' rather than 'Koz', in other words, you pronounce the name of the island like 'cross', just leaving out the 'r'. And after all this, you'll also know now the correct pronunciation of the place name Kéfalos in the west: like 'Keffaloss'. As with all multisyllabic Greek words, the accents point out which syllable the stress should fall on.

Today, the monastery of Ágios Ioánnis Pródromos is abandoned

need of propping up casts its shade over the small monastery church. ● On the terrace you'll see the first cement tables and benches. If you're wondering what they are there for, you'll see for yourself maybe if you're lucky enough to be in the area for the great church feast on 28/29 August, when the quaint square turns into a place of joyful abandon, with up to 400 pilgrims coming together to eat, drink and dance. On any other good day in summer the terrace is good for a picnic. In high season, a small *kantína* in the courtyard of the monastery sells salad, toast and drinks, as well as ☺ honey from their own bees at very reasonable prices.

There are only ruins now where the cells used to be, and the old bell in the tree in front is hardly ever rung these days. *Freely accessible | 1.5 mi past the fork to Panagía Ziniótissa, a small tarmac road branches off to the monastery, only 200 m away. 4.5 mi from Kéfalos*

LANGADES BEACH
(111 D2) (*⊞ C–D 5–6*)

Section of the eastern beach of Kéfalos with small drinks-selling operation and sunshade hire. *Access is signposted from the main road, some 500 m away.*

LIMNIÓNAS (110 C2) (*⊞ B5*)

This small port of refuge on the northern coast, sometime simply called and spelt Limiónas, was established in the 1980s. Starting right on the harbour, the 100 metres of sandy beach with a few sun loungers and sunshades don't attract many visitors; and in the neighbouring bay with its short pebble beach you might well be on your own. There is no village as such, but the only building on the harbour is the recommended *Limniónas fish restaurant*. Owner Jánnis Bézas speaks excellent English and has three fishing boats working exclusively for him. Various first courses from the sea are on the menu, the fresh fish is usually grilled on charcoal. If you see buses parked outside the restaurant, be prepared to wait, as the staff and the kitchen often struggle to cope with a large number of guests. *On the harbour | daily | Expensive*

MAGIC BEACH ⭐ (111 E2) *(∅ D5)*

This section of the long eastern beach, only accessible using a rough track, has no tavern, but a drinks stall and sun-shade hire. This is a good stepping-off point for anybody who wants to continue on foot to the part of the beach eminently suitable for nudist bathing even further east. That area starts right behind the improvised *Polémi Beach* bar with its determinedly exotic palm-tree look. *Access signposted from the main road, some 1300 m away*

PANAGÍA STYLÓTI (110 B4) *(∅ B7)*

Dedicated to the Virgin Mary, this church in a lonely landscape appears to have

been built for one day in the year only: the church feast days on 14/15 August. Inside, the little church is fairly devoid of decoration, but the cement tables and benches can accommodate over 1000 revellers. Every year, the latter enjoy the typical fair fare, i.e. chickpea soap and grilled lamb or kid goat, washed down with wine or ouzo. *1300 m off the access road to Ágios Theológos, signposted in Greek only | church key hanging above the door*

PARADISE BEACH (BUBBLE BEACH) ⭐ (111 D2) *(∅ C6)*

Scheduled buses can take you to the western part of the long eastern beach of Kéfalos. The road is asphalted, and the good connection and pretty surround-

Splendid location and a long beach are the trademarks of Paradise Beach at Kéfalos

ings mean it gets busy here; the loungers and sunshades are four rows deep in parts. The beach is suitable for any kind of watersports.

In terms of scenic beauty, this section of the coast is particularly attractive: sand covers the slopes rising up steeply behind the beach, making them look like high dunes. The eastern part of Paradise Beach is also called **INSIDER TIP** *Bubble Beach*. It owes its name to a fascinating natural phenomenon which can be enjoyed by snorkellers and divers: in the sunshine, the many bubbles rising up from the bottom of the sea sparkle like diamonds. A particularly romantic experience is a full-moon dive, when a dancing veil of luminous bubbles surrounds the swimmers.

The first thing you'll notice about the large tavern *(Expensive)* a bit above the beach is the friendly service bringing out various dishes, cakes, ice-cream and all kinds of drink. The place opens early, for breakfast. Access is signposted from the main road, 600 m away.

SUNNY BEACH (111 E2) (*ØD5*)

A tarmac road leads down to this section of the eastern beach of Kéfalos, with sun loungers and sunshades for hire. The tavern located just a little way above the beach offers two shady palm and bamboo-bedecked terraces. Access to the beach is signposted from the main road, 700 m away.

TRIPS & TOURS

The tours are marked in green in the road atlas,
the pull-out map and on the back cover

1 EXPLORE THE FLAT NORTH ON A BIKE TOUR

The length of this round trip from Kos Town to Mastichári and back is just over 30 miles. Most of the mainly flat route runs on roads with little traffic. Only short sections run on country lanes or follow the island's main road. Children however should already have some experience with cycling in traffic. There are plenty of options for fuelling up and swimming along the way.

The easiest thing to do is to hire your bike for the day directly in Kos Town → p. 86. Start off by cycling down to the port of Mandráki and take a left at the western end of the port road onto the broad cycle lane on *Odós G. Averof*. When you reach the end, turn right and follow the road running alongside the beach in a northerly direction. This leads you past what used to be an industrial estate with a former tomato puree factory converted into the popular *Kalua Club*. To dance here you have to come in summer. When you can't carry on any more, turn left following the broad main street through the quarter of Lambí to reach the sea. The most northerly point of the island is marked by the flat Kap Ammoudiá, which today houses a military base and a beacon. The long sandy beach starting right at the cape stretches from here to Mastichári, the tour's finishing point. Its route runs for the most part right along the beach, so that you can stop off for a

Whether by bike, boat or on foot –
the following routes allow you to experience
the best of Kos and its neighbouring islands

dip along the way. Sometimes it leaves the coast and goes through fields. After the grain harvest in early June all you see here is brown, burnt earth, but before that time there is an enchanting cornucopia of wild field flowers here. You can't get lost really, as long as you stay on the cycle path for as long as you can, and then always keep to the small tarmac road closest to the sea.

The first village you reach, after about 7.5 mi, is Tigáki → p. 65. At the roundabout on the beach take a right onto the

road hugging the coast, which leads you past fast-food stalls and tavernas to the *Taverna Alikes*. Now comes the only part of the route which might call for a mountain bike, after rainfalls, when conditions can get quite bad. Turn left immediately after the taverna, carry on along the eastern side, then along the entire southern side of the Alikés Saline Lake. Here, nature is pristine still. Right into spring, the saline lake offers food to INSIDER TIP flamingos and other water-fowl. If you get off your bike to taste the very salty water, take care: often, the dry-looking soil turns into a trap; right below its crust lurks moist clay, just waiting for you to sink in deep!

In the southwest corner of the saline lake turn left onto the broader track leading you back onto tarmac. Follow this to the southern edge of the resort of Marmári → p. 57. Take a left there onto the road that will bring you to the island's main road. Follow this to the right for just over a mile and turn off onto the signposted smaller road leading to Mastichári. A good mile further it is worth stopping before reaching the bend on the edge of a small hollow. Here, in a most idyllic location, stands the ancient tiny church of Ágios Geórgios Loízos under the imposing umbrella of a pine tree. This chapel is probably some 800 years old; remains of an Early Christian basilica from the 5th/6th century were recycled for its construction. The harbour at Mastichári → p. 59 makes an excellent lunch-time pit stop for food and/or a dip.

The way back into town leads you in part over roads already familiar to you, but is shorter and asphalted throughout. From Mastichári harbour, first of all follow the main road south, taking a left before you reach the end of the village, in front of a former disco. After about a mile you will meet the road that you already know, leading past the Ágios Geórgios Loízos church to the main road of the island. Follow that for about 1.5 mi, until the tiny Linopótis Pond appears to your right. It is populated by several families of ducks, and tortoises sunbathe on the rocks around its rim. After passing the pond, turn left and shortly afterwards right. To your left you'll see the Alikés saline lake again, soon reaching the road to Tigáki. Turn right here and follow the island's main road in the direction of Kos Town. Beyond the bridge immediately

following, a path leads about 100 m to the ruined Early Christian basilica of Ágios Pávlos.

You are now crossing the large modern village of Zipári → p. 69 with its modest cafés. A mile past the centre of the village you will encounter a signpost (unfortunately only readable from the other side) pointing to Ágios Ioánnis/St John Chapel. Although the chapel is locked, one can make out that it was built above an Early Christian vaulted tomb. Following the little road brings you to the road running near the coast that you know from the way out here, and which after 5.5 mi will take you back to Kos Town.

2 TAKE THE BOAT TO PICTURE-PERFECT VILLAGES AND A VOLCANO

Day trips to Níssiros are on offer from Kos Town (27 mi from the main settlement of Mandráki), Kéfalos and Kardámena. This means that you're travelling from about 9am to 5pm. It is a lot cheaper to take the trip using a scheduled boat service; however, this usually means staying the night on Níssiros. Right on the harbour there are several basic hotels, and all in all taking the scheduled boat and paying for an overnight stay won't cost more than the organised day trip.

Each Greek island is a world of its own, and while Kos is pretty, it is not necessarily a typical Greek island. Take advantage of the opportunity to go on an all-day boat trip to the southerly islet of Níssiros, seven times smaller than Kos, and see what life is like on a much smaller and less touristy island. Furthermore, travellers appreciating nature and landscapes will find on Níssiros what art lovers would find at the Acropolis in Athens: one of the top sights!

Only some 1000 people live on Níssiros, distributed over four villages. Tour boats and ferries moor at the jetty of the main settlement, **Mandráki**, which stretches across a few hundred metres along the sea to a castle erected by the Knights of St John on a rocky cape. The way there also passes the tiny beach of Mandráki with its small playground. Often lucky visitors may find feather-light ● pumice stone, which is washed across by the sea from the mining island of **Gialí** opposite. The church on the castle compound is dedicated to the Virgin Mary and is a very popular pilgrimage destination during the first half of August. In the tavernas along the shore you are sitting right above the sea; no less pretty is the elongated INSIDER TIP village square further inland, where the tables and chairs of several cafés and restaurants have been set up under tall trees.

However, a stroll through the village is not the real highlight of the trip. For this you need to take one of the buses waiting at the port. These wind their way uphill on the narrow streets of the island to the edge of the crater. This is where you suddenly realise that Níssiros is hollow inside: steep slopes up

The ruins of a castle erected by the Knights of St John watch over Mandráki

to 2290 ft high surround a deep crater, two miles long and half a mile wide, its floor lying only about 100 to 200 metres above sea level. One half is so green that even cows graze on it, but the other resembles a lunar landscape because it has been carved out by another crater about 350 m long and 250 m wide. The rocks on the bottom of the crater are so hot that you could fry eggs on them in a matter of minutes. Sulphuric vapours rise from several places, and often you can see bright yellow sulphur deposits. A further four secondary craters nearby are hard to get to.

Looking up from the bottom of the crater to the crater's edge, you will spot two small villages up there: Nikiá and Embório. One part of the population looks out of their windows right into the crater, another looks down to the sea. This is something you will find only in one other place in Greece, on the much more famous island of Santorini. A day trip doesn't leave enough time to visit Nikiá and Embório. Staying overnight on Níssiros gives you the chance to hire a moped or car and drive up there. When you get to Nikiá, a small modern *museum* has information on volcanism *(Sat–Thu 11am–3pm | admission 2 euros)*.

3 CRUISE FROM ISLAND TO ISLAND BY SAILING BOAT

A whole day to laze around, swim and discover the island. Duration of the trip: from around 9.30am to 5.30pm, various operators. Travellers who don't want to go with a tour might save money through booking directly with the boat; this means losing out on the transfer from hotel to port.

A number of large sailing boats promote their Three Islands tours, which all offer the same programme. The sails are only set for atmosphere and to please photographers really; propulsion is by motor engines. Still, the tour is an ideal mix of a relaxed experience and a short encounter with two more Greek islands.

The first stop is usually the 6.5 sq mi islet of Psérimos between Kos and the Turkish coast. In the summer, about 130 people live on the island, in winter this dwindles to 20. There are hardly any cars and no tarmac roads. The pretty sandy beach at the inner end of the narrow bay, sheltering the only village on the island, represents its main drag. The only sight as such is the Kímissis tis Theotókou church erected in 1830, which stands amidst a paradisiacal garden which nominally belongs to the Virgin Mary. A few rooms are available for rent on the beach, and it's all too easy to lose track of time in the local tavernas. The pleasure boats set sail again after just one hour's stay in order to head across to the sponge fishing island of Kálimnos. The boats anchor in the large port of the island capital of Póthia, just under 20 mi from Kos Town. Kálimnos is not even half the size of Kos and much of it is rocky and barren. Today, only about 16,500 people still live here, most of them in Póthia. The locals dedicate themselves to fishing, catching swordfish in particular, cultivate tangerines and make a little money from tourism, which however is concentrated in a few places on the western coast.

The island capital comes across as quite wealthy, being the centre of Greek sponge fishing in the 19th century and the second half of the 20th century. Today, only about 30 boats launch diving expeditions in late spring. In the olden days the sponge fishers worked the seas all summer, going all the way to the coasts of North Africa and only returning in the autumn. Artificial sponges have spelt a commercial downturn, and

Kálimnos is worth a visit, and not only for the sponges

hunting for sponges is mainly limited to Greek waters.

Despite all this, Póthia has remained a centre of sponge processing. However, today you find not only Kalymnian sponges on offer, but increasingly Caribbean sponges as well. In various shops along the coastal road and in the alleyways behind it you can see how the sponges are cleaned and graded, and of course buy them too. If you buy, check they have an even texture and no signs of having been cut. INSIDER TIP Good-quality sponges are round and convex, never squeezed flat. On some autumn days parts of the shore promenade are completely covered in sponges, when the catches of the Kalymnian fishermen are spread out to dry in the sun.

On the way back from Kálimnos to Kos, the sailing boats set anchor in a bay off the uninhabited rock island of Pláti. While the guests can step into the water to swim or snorkel, the crew put together a simple meal.

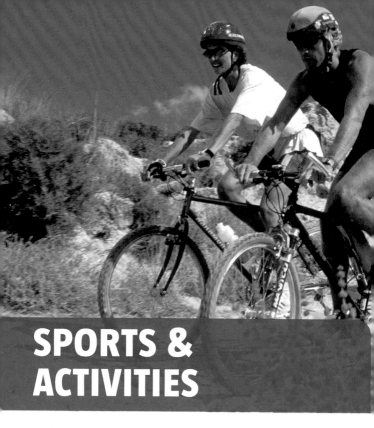

SPORTS & ACTIVITIES

Kos is a good destination for an activity holiday; there are plenty of options for water sports enthusiasts in particular. Windsurfers appreciate the short distances, giving them a flexible choice of launch area depending on the way the wind blows.

As is the case everywhere in Greece, the options offered by water sports centres depend on the season. If you're visiting out of season, it is best to contact the individual providers beforehand.

BIKING

Thanks to a large number – by Greek standards – of cycle paths and gentle ascents, Kos is ideally suited to cycling. Many beach hotels and independent stations hire out touring and mountain bikes. A recommended, centrally located station with a large choice of well-kept bikes at good-value rates is Moto Holidays in Kos Town (Odós Meg. Aléxandrou 2 | tel. 22 42 02 86 76).

The Dutch-Greek company *Moto Harley* has a branch in town, but also along the main roads of Lambí and Psalídi: *Odós Kanari 42/Ecke Odós Neomártiros Christoú | Kos Town | tel. 22 42 02 76 93; Lambí: tel. 22 42 02 00 61; Psalídi: tel. 22 42 02 76 93*

CLIMBING

Connoisseurs appreciate Kálimnos,

From B for Biking to Y for Yoga – Kos offers active holidaymakers a vast range of options

the neighbouring island of Kos, as an INSIDER TIP excellent destination for climbers, who particularly value its proximity to the sea, the short drives to the climbing areas and the stable climate. Signposts on the roadside point to the climbing routes. The municipality has published a route guide, and many guesthouses have specific information available for climbers. The season lasts for the entire year. General information can be found online at *www.kalymnosisl.gr/climb;* specific questions can be answered on site by the *Official Climbing Info Desk* on the coastal road in Kastélli *(Mon–Fri 8.30am–1.30pm).*

DIVING

The underwater world of Bubble Beach alone makes it worth thinking about going for a dive. The fascinating bubbling water becomes visible in shallow water and may be admired using simple equipment. Snorkelling is permitted in all waters around Kos. Fish may only be harpooned of their length is 25 cm upwards. Scuba diving is only allowed at a few specific places, and only when accompanied by licensed diving instructors. The INSIDER TIP *Liámis Dive Centre* aboard the MS Apollon, which sets anchor at night at Mandráki harbour, offers classes and all kinds of accompanied dives. *Office Odós Mandilára 67 | tel. 69 44 29 58 30 | www.liamisdivecentre.com | onboard information daily 7–10pm*

GYM

Gym equipment with sea views is drawing more and more young Koans into the *Fitness Village* on the coastal road east of the castle. Free WiFi allows a quick email check in between sessions. *Odós Vas. Georgíou/Odós Arseníou 2 | tel. 69 48 75 40 70 | Mon–Fri 8am–11pm*

HIKING

Kos is not really suited to a proper hiking holiday. However, recommended day hikes are available on the Kéfalos peninsula and on the slopes of Mount Díkeos between Asklípion, Zía and Old Pýli. The summit of Díkeos requires no mountaineering skills either.

There are however no hiking maps or signposted hiking trails. For an overview, consult the 1:60 000 map of Kos published by the Greek publishers Road Edition, which is available on Amazon, for example. Thorny scrub makes wearing long trousers a good idea. Sturdy footwear is a must, and don't forget a sunhat and to carry water.

HORSE RIDING

Kos has two riding stables. INSIDER TIP *Alfa Horse* is geared towards both beginners and experienced riders, leads tours into the mountains and offers things like dressage classes. The owners strive to give their animals the best possible conditions. *Salt Lake Riding* offers mainly easy tours and beach rides. *Alfa Horse | Amanioú (in Amanioú, coming from Pýli take a left before the church, then a right on the first asphalted road) | tel. 22 42 04 19 08 | www.alfahorse.com; Salt Lake Riding Center Gina Daoúlas | on the road to Chrístos Go Karts between Marmári and Tigáki towards the coast | mobile 69 44 10 44 46*

TENNIS

While there are no public tennis courts on the island, many of the larger beach hotels have courts which are open to non-residents too.

WATER SPORTS

Water sports centres with a large range of activities can be found mainly in larger hotels on the northern coast, in Kéfalos Bay, on the beaches of Kardámena and at Paradise Beach. These operations offer water skiing, windsurfing, paragliding, jet skiing and Fun Rides. There are opportunities for Hobie Cat sailing on the beach in front of the Caravia Beach hotel east of Marmári, as well as on Kéfalos Bay. The best area for windsurfing on the northern coast lies between Marmári and Tigáki. A wind channel between the sandy beach and Psérimos island opposite creates ideal conditions for all levels. This is where the international team working at ★ *Caravia Beach Watersports*

Centre offers courses in windsurfing, dinghy and catamaran sailing, as well as water skiing. *Tel. 22 42 04 19 26 or tel. 22 42 04 12 91 (hotel reception) | mobile 69 44 55 84 05 | mid-April–Oct | www. caravia-wassersport.de*

Kéfalos Bay offers excellent conditions for speedsurfing, with mostly cross-offshore winds. The morning is ideal for beginners, the afternoon for the pros. One long-established station is run by Swiss Jens and his partner Lynn on Skála beach: *Kéfalos Windsurfing | tel. 22 42 07 17 27 | www. kefaloswindsurfing.com*

Specialising in the trend sport of kitesurfing, Yiánnis Antonoúris operates from Kochilári Beach northeast of Kéfalos. *Kefalos Kitesurfing | tel. 69 32 47 40 93 | www.kefalos.com/kefaloskitesurfing*

YACHT CHARTERS

Sailing ● yachts can be rented on a daily or weekly basis, with the relevant yachting permits a requirement. Sometimes private skippers on the port of Mandráki and in Kos Town's marina offer the chance to hitch a ride on their yacht; look for notices pinned up on the boats. There is a small provider on Kos and a larger one on the neighbouring island of Kálimnos: *Istíon | Kos Marina | tel. 22 42 02 21 95 | www.istion.com; Kálymna Yachting | Póthia | tel. 22 43 02 40 83 | www.kalymna-yachting.gr*

YOGA

While Kos is not exactly a hotspot on the yoga circuit, you can still have a yoga holiday here, courtesy of a British provider working from the ● Pántheon hotel at Kéfalos. *Kos Yoga | tel. 0044 16 84 54 08 76 | www.kosyoga.com*

Windsurfers enjoy good conditions

TRAVEL WITH KIDS

For families with children, Kos is an uncomplicated destination. Kids are welcome not only in resort facilities specialising in families, but everywhere. The Greeks themselves don't make a big fuss over children, but let them participate in nearly everything that the adults do – way beyond midnight.

A wide choice of basics such as baby food, nappies and fresh milk can be got from larger supermarkets. Hopefully you will never need them, but experienced paediatricians have set up surgeries in Kos Town. In terms of splashing about and taking dips, children who aren't confident swimmers are much better served by the flat beaches on the northern coast than by those in the south. The latter shelve more steeply down to deeper waters, and there is often a bit of a swell too. Swim shoes, available for little money on Kos in many shops and in all sizes, are handy for adults and even more so for children. Not only do they make it easier to reach the water walking on gravel or pebbles, they also protect from the often burning-hot sand in summer and painful encounters with a sea urchin. Most larger hotels have a splash pool. And families living in a hotel or apartment with no pool are usually able to use the hotel pools if buying drinks and snacks from the pool bar. Discounts are available to children up to twelve years of age in

Attractions for young travellers – tips and ideas for family activities that guarantee a big deal for the little ones

buses, on ferries and tour boats, as well as at many events. The age assessment is handled quite generously, hardly anybody wants to see ID.

KOS TOWN

EXCAVATIONS
(U B–C 4–5) (ⵍ b–c 4–5)
The archaeological sites in Kos town are very child-friendly indeed, particularly the western zone. In contrast to the vast majority of sites in Greece there are no guards waiting to blow their whistle at visitors leaving the designated paths. Many walls great and small may be climbed, giving creative parents the chance to send their kids on a time travel trip to antiquity. Just declare one of the ruins your very own home, sort out who gets which room and let your children cook you a meal. This might give you

some breathing space while they whip up imaginary delicacies from grasses and flowers and then call you to the dinner table.

TRIPS ON THE CHOOCHOO TRAIN
(U C–D4) (*ⓜ c–d4*)
Trenáki, small train, is what the Greek call the breezy electrified trains with a locomotive and two or three open carriages on rubber wheels plying the roads of many Greek holiday resorts. Kos boasts three of those. One starts from the Mandráki port of the island capital on roughly 20-minute tours of the town, the other hourly from the central bus station on the shore road east of the castle, for a slightly longer trip to Asklípion, sadly without stopping in Platáni. Child-friendly fun background music is provided too. A third *trenáki* runs in Kardámena on the island's southern coast.

THE CENTRE

INSIDER TIP GO KARTS FOR ANY AGE
☺ (113 E1) (*ⓜ G2*)
Many holiday islands boast go-kart tracks, but *Chrístos Go Karts* at Marmári goes one step further and thinks of the little ones too. While the adults hare through the bends on their heavily horse-powered karts, three to eight-year olds can go round and round on a separate track on eco-friendlier electric karts. *Chrístos Go Karts Marmári | daily 9am–11pm | large karts approx. 18 euros/ 20 min, electro karts approx. 4 euros/8 min.*

DONKEY OR MULE – YOU CHOOSE
(113 F3) (*ⓜ G–H3*)
The unique chance for children to ride a donkey or mule comes at the foot of Old Pýli's castle hill. Between June and mid-September the animals wait to carry small and larger guests up to the *Café*

Ória. The café's outdoor tables and chairs allow for enough space to frolic around. Just one thing: the café is only open in good weather.

WATERY FUN ON GIANT SLIDES
(113 D2) (*ⓜ F3*)
Several giant slides, large pools and a Lazy River are the main attractions offered by the 20-acre *Lido Water Park* between Marmári and Mastichári. *On the coastal road between the two villages | mid-May–early Oct, daily 10am–7pm | adults approx. 20 euros, children (3–12 years) approx. 12 euros | www.lidowaterpark.com*

TAVERNAS WITH PLAYGROUND
(112 B–C2) (*ⓜ E3*)
A familiar dilemma: the parents would like to enjoy some food and chat in peace and quiet, the children want to frolic and play. Two tavernas in and near Mastichári help to solve the problem. In the *Traditional Greek House* on the edge of Mastichári the older generation may stay seated on the terrace to keep an eye on their children playing on the sandy municipal playground right in front of the eatery. And at *Tam Tam* east of Mastichári the fenced-in taverna lawn is so generously sized that the kids can even play ball games while their parents enjoy the fine cooking, the hushed music and sea view.

INSIDER TIP HORSE RIDING CLASSES FOR CHILDREN ☺ (113 E2–3) (*ⓜ G3*)
The Alfa Horse stables near the mountain village of Pýli offers English-language riding tuition as well as hacks for children with some horse-riding experience. Helmets are available. The stables house child-friendly mounts ranging from Welsh to Shetland ponies. *Alfa Horse | Amanioú/Pýli (off the road leading from*

If you ask children, they'd choose the sea as their favourite destination without fail; on the beach, there's always something to do

Amanioú to Zía; in Amanioú turn left in front of the church coming from Pýli, then take a right at the first asphalted road) | tel. 22 42 04 19 08 | www.alfa-horse.com

WINDSURFING COURSES FOR YOUNGSTERS (113 E1) (*ØØ G2*)

The *Caravia Beach* water sports centre on the beach in front of the hotel of the same name near Marmári runs windsurfing courses specifically designed for children from about ten years up. Training advances in steps appropriate for children, using material especially adapted to younger learners. Should the kids wish to carry on practising after the daily classes (a course takes between ten to twelve hours usually) students have access to board and rig free of charge. *Course fee approx. 140 euros, exam fee around 30*

euros. Water sports centre Holger Bründel | Caravia Beach | tel. 22 42 04 19 26 | mobile tel. 69 44 55 84 05 | www.caravia-wassersport.de

THE WEST

ADVENTURES FOR SMALL SWIMMERS (111 D3) (*ØØ C6*)

The islet of Kastrí right off Ágios Stéfanos beach is fairly easily accessible from the shore by a combination of swimming and wading. Accompanied by adults, even small children who only manage a few lengths are able to complete the passage safely. Two cords held in place by buoys (to keep away motor boats and windsurfers) offer something to hold on to if the little ones should get a bit tired.

FESTIVALS & EVENTS

Compared to other Aegean islands, there are fewer parties on Kos. There are fewer villages and in the summer, there is a lot of work. However, the village saints have to be honoured, so the tradition of church feast days is upheld. The festivities often begin on the eve of the holiday proper, with music and dance. On the day itself often only a religious service is held. The year's most important feast day is Easter, whose date as for all moveable holidays follows the Julian calendar. This means that they rarely coincide with our the religious holidays of the same name celebrated by Western Christian churches.

PUBLIC HOLIDAYS

1 Jan *New Year*; **6 Jan** *Epiphany*; **25 March** *National Holiday*; **1 May** *Labour Day*; **15 Aug** *Dormition of the Virgin Mary*; **28 Oct** *National Holiday*; **25/26 Dec** *Christmas*

MOVEABLE FEASTS

Carnival Monday 27 February 2012, 18 March 2013; **Good Friday** 13 April 2012, 3 May 2013; **Easter** 15/16 April 2012, 5/6 May 2013; **Whitsun** 3/4 June 2012, 23/24 June 2013

FESTIVALS & EVENTS

FEBRUARY
▶ **1/2 Feb:** Traditional *church feast day* in the ruined village of *Old Pýli*

FEBRUARY/MARCH
▶ **Carnival Monday:** the Koans enjoy outdoor picnics and fly kites. In the small ● Pláka forest near the airport, a popular picnic spot all year round, a lot of barbecues take place.

MARCH
▶ **25 March:** *National holiday* commemorating the Greek uprising against Turkish dominion 1821

APRIL/MAI
INSIDERTIP ▶ *Church feast day* Fun takes centre stage at the horseracing held in the afternoon along the main street in the lower part of *Pýli*. As there is heavy betting, a good few people take an interest in who wins (next dates: 23 April 2012, 6 May 2013).
▶ **Good Friday:** in the morning, in all churches the symbolic grave of Christ is decorated with countless flowers. Over the course of the day believers crawl below the colourful contraption; this act

The island's calendar of events is dominated by religious festivals and holidays with much music, dancing and folklore

of contrition is supposed to bring good luck for the coming year. Towards 9pm there are processions in all the towns and villages

▶ **Easter Saturday:** Easter Mass at 11pm is a fixture for nearly all Koans. Shortly before midnight, all lights go out in the churches, leaving only the eternal flame. Around midnight, the priest proclaims the resurrection of Christ. Everybody in the church lights candles, and outside, the youngsters stage noisy fireworks with firecrackers and rockets.

▶ **Easter Sunday :** everywhere, lambs or kid goats are turning on the spit. Another equally popular tradition is to carve up the Easter lamb and to let it slowly cook all night in a clay or stone oven.

JULI

▶ **26 July:** Antimáchia fortress: a *religious service* in the *Agía Paraskeví* is followed by a solemn procession.

AUGUST

▶ ★ The entire month is given over to ★ *Ippokratía*, a series of concerts, theatre and folklore performances organised by the municipal administration together with many cultural associations. Events are held on the open-air stages in the castle of the Knights of St John at the port, the Odeon and the town's stadium. Exact details are usually released at quite short notice; the tourist information has the details.

▶ **14/15 August:** *major church feast* in Kéfalos. Much folklore, music and dance

▶ **28/29 Aug.:** *church feast* with music and dancing in Kardámena and at the Ágios Ioánnis Pródromos monastery on the Kéfalos peninsula. The busiest time is on the eve of 28 Aug after the service is over.

SEPTEMBER

▶ **14 Sept:** in the morning a *religious service* is held in the tiny chapel above the grave of Harmylos in *Pýli*

LINKS, BLOGS, APPS & MORE

LINKS

▶ www.koswireless.gr/en List of all free WiFi hotspots provided by the municipality of Kos with the relevant Google Maps reference

▶ www.photokos.gr On his homepage, photographer Panagiótis Grigoríou presents over 1000 images of Kos. Well worth checking out!

▶ www.kosinfo.gr Extensive webpage with information, photographs, videos, webcams and weather data

▶ www.animals.cos-island.info Homepage of the island's animal activists. If you need a vet or would like to adopt one of the stray dogs here, this is the website for you

▶ www.greenmaven.com The ‚Gateway to the Green Web' uses Google's search engine to filter green content from web links; put in ‚Kos' and ‚Greece' as search terms.

▶ www.fanatic-boarderscenter.com/en/destinations/home/2 The site of a local windsurf school is worth consulting for wind charts, photographs and other information

▶ http://www.travel-to-kos.com Commercial webpage with videos, eCards and much more

BLOGS & FORUMS

▶ www.tripadvisor.co.uk The well-established review website has the up-to-date lowdown on tourist infrastructure and an active forum on topics such as getting married on Kos

▶ www.kosradio.gr This music portal offers information on events on the island while streaming non-stop dance music

▶ www.kosinfo.gr/en/multimedia/kos-videos Webcams and a collection of official tourism videos – some of them unintentionally comical

VIDEOS, STREAMS & PODCASTS

▶ www.vimeo.com/user1209121 The Kos Team guys don't share anything with the Greek island apart from the name, but their windsurf and kite-boarding videos are pretty cool

▶ www.vimeo.com/6038881 A fun experiment: the surroundings of Marmári, filmed with a mobile camera mounted on a bike

▶ http://www.youtube.com/watch?v=aYqfJKK9SFQ Like diving in a jacuzzi: watch the famous release of underground gases at Bubble Beach near Kéfalos

APPS

▶ Mastichari Bay Hotel Apart from information on the hotel itself, this app offers other useful information, such as integrated maps, phone number and addresses, as well as the weather forecast. iPhone, English

▶ iSlands makes island hopping and trip planning easier. The pre-set port names facilitate the search. iPhone, Greek/English

▶ Best Hippocrates works Bookworms and fans of Hippocrates may upload 17 works in English by the Father of Medicine onto your iPhone. A search function allows you to scour the eBook for key words

NETWORKS

▶ www.justkos.co.uk Very active community exchanging their experiences with car hire firms, hotels, bars or restaurants on the island.

▶ www.facebook.com/profile.php?id=100000011544384 The facebook page of the Status Club in Kardámena has over 3000 fans, who publish photos of party nights. Just ask them to be your Friend!

▶ www.twitter.com/kosisland The Twitter page of the Kos municipality spreads the odd bit of local news

TRAVEL TIPS

ADMISSION CHARGES

All state-run museums and archaeological sites offer free entrance to children and adolescents from EU countries, as well as to students in possession of their international student card; senior citizens over 65 enjoy a discount.

ARRIVAL

Direct flights, including various budget carriers, connect Kos between May and October with numerous airports in English-speaking countries. There are also connections several times a day between Athens and Kos, e. g. by *Olympic Air (www.olympicair.com)*, *Athens Airways (www.athensairways.com)* and *Aegean Airlines (www.aegeanair.com)*. There is no problem getting a taxi from the airport.

The land/sea route always involves Piraeus, from where there is at least one car ferry a day to Kos. These ferries usually run at night, taking some 8–11 hours for the trip.

BANKS & MONEY

ATMs (cash points) accept the major debit and credit cards. Traveller's cheques can be cashed in banks and post offices. *Opening times of the banks: Mon–Thu 8am–2pm, Fri 8am–1.30pm*

BUSES

Scheduled buses are the most important public transport option on the island and offer the best value. Even the longest distance (Kos Town–Kéfalos) costs no more than around 4 euros. We have listed more exact information on all scheduled bus connections on the pages with the relevant place descriptions.

CAR HIRE

A large selection of bikes, mopeds, scooters, motorbikes and cars may be rented in any holiday resort. To rent a car or a motorbike over 125 cm³ you will need the national drivers' licence for the relevant category and have to be at least 21 years of age. Even taking out the fully comprehensive insurance doesn't insure you against damage to the tyres or the undercarriage of the vehicle. Do call the police after even the tiniest accident, as the insurance won't pay otherwise. Maximum speed in built-up areas is 50 km/h, on country roads 90 km/h. Seatbelts have to be worn on the front seats. The blood alcohol limits for drivers are 50mg of alcohol per 100ml of blood, for motorbikers and caravanners 10mg! Parking offences are a costly affair on Kos, as the fines start at 60 euros.

RESPONSIBLE TRAVEL

It doesn't take a lot to be environmentally friendly whilst travelling. Don't just think about your carbon footprint whilst flying to and from your holiday destination but also about how you can protect nature and culture abroad. As a tourist it is especially important to respect nature, look out for local products, cycle instead of driving, save water and much more. If you would like to find out more about eco-tourism please visit: www.ecotourism.org

From arrival to weather

Holiday from start to finish: the most important addresses and information for your Kos trip

CLIMATE, WHEN TO GO

The season on Kos lasts from May to October. Outside that time most hotels and restaurants outside the capital are closed. In May the water might be a bit cool for swimming, but nature is at its best, with beautiful blossoms everywhere. In July and August the mercury rises well over 30 degrees Celsius/86 Fahrenheit, hardly ever sinking below 20 degrees C/68 F. The autumn offers the advantage of pleasantly warm swimming temperatures, but the disadvantage of a largely withered and burnt vegetation. There is hardly any rain between June and September; even so, bring a light rain jacket for any thundershowers. In the height of summer there are often strong winds that can cool too, so a light jacket or jumper should go into your suitcase.

CLUBS

Greek discos don't really open until 11pm or midnight. While there is usually no entrance charge, the drinks can set you back a bit (for instance, a cocktail costs around 7–9 euros, a small bottle of beer 4–6 euros).

CONSULATES AND EMBASSIES

There are no consulates on Kos; any queries need to be addressed to the embassies of your country in Athens.

BRITISH EMBASSY
Odós Ploutarchou 106 | 75 Athens | tel. 21 07 27 2 600 | www.ukingreece.fco.gov.uk

US EMBASSY
Vasilisis Sophias Avenue 91 | 10160 Athens | tel. 21 07 21 29 51 | www.athens.usembassy.gov

CUSTOMS

EU citizens may import and export duty-free goods for personal use, incl. 800 cigarettes, 10 l of spirits and 90 l of wine. For North American citizens the quantities are lower: 220 cigarettes and 2 l of still wine or 1 l of spirits.

ELECTRICITY

220-volt alternating current; bring a three-to-two pin adapter.

HEALTH

All larger settlements on the island have a pharmacy. In an emergency, hospital treatment is free of charge. European citizens can get tree treatment from state-registered doctors on showing their European Health Card issued by state-backed insurers. However, used to being tipped, Greek doctors are not too keen on treating foreigners as part of

BUDGETING

Coffee	2 euros	*for a cup of mocha*
Beer	3 euros	*for half a litre*
Snack	2.10 euros	*for a gýros*
Beach	4–7 euros	*for 2 sun loungers*
Bike	from 4 euros	*per day*
Taxi	1.36 euros	*per kilometre*

this arrangement. A travel health policy helps avoid any problems.

IMMIGRATION

A valid passport or European ID card is sufficient documentation. Children under 12 need to have their own child's passport.

INFORMATION

GREEK TOURIST BOARDS

Greek National Tourism Organisation UK/ Ireland: 4 Conduit Street | London W1S 2DJ, tel. 020 74 95 93 00 | www.visitgreece.gr; USA: Olympic Tower 645, Fifth Av., Suite 903, New York, NY 10022 | tel. 212 4 21 57 77 | gnto@greektourism.com | Canada: 1500

Don Mills Road, suite 102 | Toronto, ON | tel. 41 69 68 22 20 | grnto.tor@on.atbn.com

INTERNET CAFÉS & WIFI

Many hotels and cafés offer free WiFi access hotspots to guests with their own laptop. Payable internet terminals can be found in some travel agencies. Most internet cafés are in heavy demand from young locals for playing computer games.

NEWSPAPERS

Foreign daily newspapers can usually be had on the day of publication. English-language news from Kos is only available online: *www.kosexplorer.com.*

WEATHER ON KOS

	Jan.	Feb.	March	April	May	June	July	Aug.	Sept.	Oct.	Nov.	Dec.
Daytime temperatures in °C/°F												
	15/59	16/61	17/63	21/70	25/77	30/86	32/90	33/91	29/84	25/77	21/70	17/63
Nighttime temperatures in °C/°F												
	7/45	8/46	9/48	11/52	15/59	19/66	21/70	22/72	19/66	15/59	12/54	9/48
Sunshine hours/day												
	5	5	7	9	10	12	13	12	11	8	6	4
Precipitation days/month												
	14	10	8	3	3	0	0	0	1	6	7	13
Water temperature in °C/°F												
	17/63	16/61	16/61	17/63	19/66	21/70	23/73	25/77	24/75	22/72	20/68	18/64

NUDISM

While officially banned in Greece, nudism is practiced on many remote beaches.

PHONE & MOBILE PHONE

The OTE telecommunications provider has offices in all the main towns and villages on Kos, from where you can make phone calls. Phone cards with 100 units are available there too, as well as from many kiosks. When you first buy a Greek SIM card (approx. 5 euros) with a Greek phone number, you need to show a passport, then you'll immediately be issued with a number. Save on roaming costs by choosing the least expensive network. Be careful around the east of the island: mobiles have a tendency to dial into the network of an expensive Turkish provider. Dialling codes: *UK: 0044 | Ireland: 00353 | US/Canada: 001 | Greece: 0030 |*

POST

There are post offices in all towns and larger villages. Opening times are *Monday to Fridays between 7.30am and 3pm*. A postcard home will take about 2–3 days, longer for North America.

PRICES

Prices are not much below UK or US level. Generally, overnight stays and public transport are much cheaper, groceries and petrol substantially more expensive.

TAXIS

About 70 taxis operate on Kos, all metered. You can either stop one on the road, join at taxi stands or call one out by phone, for an extra charge of about 3 euros. Prices are fixed by the state and relatively low; a taxi from the airport into Kos Town costs about 35 euros.

TIME

In Greece, it's an hour later than in the UK and Ireland all year round. The changeover between summer and winter time happens on the same day in all EU countries. The time difference to the US and Canada varies between 7 and 10 hours.

TIPPING

A general rounding-up as elsewhere in Europe is fine; tips of US or even UK size are not expected.

CURRENCY CONVERTER

£	€	€	£
1	1.10	1	0.90
3	3.30	3	2.70
5	5.50	5	4.50
13	14.30	13	11.70
40	44	40	36
75	82.50	75	67.50
120	132	120	108
250	275	250	225
500	550	500	450

$	€	€	$
1	0.70	1	1.40
3	2.10	3	4.20
5	3.50	5	7
13	9.10	13	18.20
40	28	40	56
75	52.50	75	105
120	84	120	168
250	175	250	350
500	350	500	700

For current exchange rates see www.xe.com

USEFUL PHRASES GREEK

PRONUNCIATION

We have provided a simple pronunciation aid for the Greek words
(see middle column). Note the following:

'   the following syllable is emphasised
ð   in Greek (shown as "dh" in middle column) is like "th" in "there"
θ   in Greek (shown as "th" in middle column) is like "th" in "think"
X   in Greek (shown as "ch" in middle column) is like a rough "h" or
    "ch" in Scottish "loch"

A	α	a	H	η	i	N	ν	n	T	τ	t
B	β	v	Θ	θ	th	Ξ	ξ	ks, x	Y	υ	i, y
Γ	γ	g, y	I	ι	i, y	O	o	o	Φ	φ	f
Δ	δ	th	K	κ	k	Π	π	p	X	χ	ch
E	ε	e	Λ	λ	l	P	ρ	r	Ψ	ψ	ps
Z	ζ	z	M	μ	m	Σ	σ, ς s, ss		Ω	ω	o

IN BRIEF

Yes/No/Maybe	ne/'ochi/'issos	Ναι/ Όχι/Ίσως
Please/Thank you	paraka'lo/efcharis'to	Παρακαλώ/Ευχαριστώ
Sorry	sig'nomi	Συγνώμη
Excuse me	me sig'chorite	Με συγχωρείτε
May I ...?	epi'treppete ...?	Επιτρέπεται …?
Pardon?	o'riste?	Ορίστε?
I would like to .../	'thelo .../	Θέλω …/
have you got ...?	'echete ...?	Έχετε …?
How much is ...?	'posso 'kani ...?	Πόσο κάνει …?
I (don't) like this	Af'to (dhen) mu a'ressi	Αυτό (δεν) μου αρέσει
good/bad	ka'llo/kak'ko	καλό/κακό
too much/much/little	'para pol'li/pol'li/'ligo	πάρα πολύ/πολύ/λίγο
everything/nothing	ólla/'tipottal	όλα/τίποτα
Help!/Attention!/	vo'ithia!/prosso'chi!/	Βοήθεια!/Προσοχή!/
Caution!	prosso'chi!	Προσοχή!
ambulance	astheno'forro	Ασθενοφόρο
police/	astino'mia/	Αστυνομία/
fire brigade	pirosvesti'ki	Πυροσβεστική
ban/	apa'gorefsi/	Απαγόρευση/
forbidden	apago'revete	απαγορεύεται
danger/dangerous	'kindinoss/epi'kindinoss	Κίνδυνος/επικίνδυνος

Milás elliniká?

"Do you speak Greek?" This guide will help you to say the basic words and phrases in Greek.

GREETINGS, FAREWELL

Good morning!/after-noon!/evening!/night!	kalli'mera/kalli'mera!/ kalli'spera!/kalli'nichta!	Καλημέρα/Καλημέρα!/ Καλησπέρα!/Καληνύχτα!
Hello!/	'ya (su/sass)!/a'dio!/	Γεία (σου/σας)!/αντίο!/
goodbye!	ya (su/sass)!	Γεία (σου/σας)!
Bye!	me 'lene ...	Με λένε ...
My name is ...	poss sass 'lene?	Πως σας λένε?

DATE & TIME

Monday/Tuesday	dhef'tera/'triti	Δευτέρα/Τρίτη
Wednesday/Thursday	tet'tarti/'pempti	Τετάρτη/Πέμπτη
Friday/Saturday	paraske'vi/'savatto	Παρασκευή/Σάββατο
Sunday/weekday	kiria'ki/er'gassimi	Κυριακή/Εργάσιμη
today/tomorrow/yesterday	'simera/'avrio/chtess	Σήμερα/Αύριο/Χτες
What time is it?	ti 'ora 'ine?	Τι ώρα είναι?

TRAVEL

open/closed	annik'ta/klis'to	Ανοικτό/Κλειστό
entrance/	'issodhos/	Είσοδος/
driveway	'issodhos ochi'matonn	Είσοδος οχημάτων
exit/exit	'eksodhos/	Έξοδος/
	'Eksodos ochi'matonn	Έξοδος οχημάτων
departure/	anna'chorissi/	Αναχώρηση/
departure/arrival	anna'chorissi/'afiksi	Αναχώρηση/Άφιξη
toilets/restrooms / ladies/	tual'lettes/gine'konn/	Τουαλέτες/Γυναικών/
gentlemen	an'dronn	Ανδρών
(no) drinking water	'possimo ne'ro	Πόσιμο νερό
Where is ...?/Where are ...?	pu 'ine ...?/pu 'ine ...?	Πού είναι/Πού είναι ...?
bus/taxi	leofo'rio/tak'si	Λεωφορείο/Ταξί
street map/	'chartis tis 'pollis/	Χάρτης της πόλης/
map	'chartis	Χάρτης
harbour	li'mani	Λιμάνι
airport	a-ero'drommio	Αεροδρόμιο
schedule/ticket	drommo'logio/issi'tirio	Δρομολόγιο/Εισιτήριο
I would like to rent ...	'thelo na nik'yasso ...	Θέλω να νοικιάσω ...
a car/a bicycle/	'enna afto'kinito/'enna	ένα αυτοκίνητο/ένα
a boat	po'dhilato/'mia 'varka	ποδήλατο/μία βάρκα
petrol/gas station	venzi'nadiko	Βενζινάδικο
petrol/gas / diesel	ven'zini/'diesel	Βενζίνη/Ντίζελ

FOOD & DRINK

Could you please book a table for tonight for four?	Klis'te mass parakal'lo 'enna tra'pezi ya a'popse ya 'tessera 'atoma	Κλείστε μας παρακαλώ ένα τραπέζι γιά απόψε γιά τέσσερα άτομα
The menu, please	tonn ka'taloggo parakal'lo	Τον κατάλογο παρακαλώ
Could I please have ...?	tha 'ithella na 'echo ...?	Θα ήθελα να έχο ...?
with/without ice/ sparkling	me/cho'ris 'pago/ anthrakik'ko	με/χωρίς πάγο/ ανθρακικό
vegetarian/allergy	chorto'fagos/allerg'ia	Χορτοφάγος/Αλλεργία
May I have the bill, please?	'thel'lo na pli'rosso parakal'lo	Θέλω να πληρώσω παρακαλώ

SHOPPING

Where can I find...?	pu tha vro ...?	Που θα βρω ...?
pharmacy/ chemist	farma'kio/ ka'tastima	Φαρμακείο/Κατάστημα καλλυντικών
bakery/market	'furnos/ago'ra	Φούρνος/Αγορά
grocery	pandopo'lio	Παντοπωλείο
kiosk	pe'riptero	Περίπτερο
expensive/cheap/price	akri'vos/fti'nos/ti'mi	ακριβός/φτηνός/Τιμή
more/less	pio/li'gotere	πιό/λιγότερο

ACCOMMODATION

I have booked a room	'kratissa 'enna do'matio	Κράτησα ένα δωμάτιο
Do you have any ... left?	'echete a'komma ...	Έχετε ακόμα ...
single room	mon'noklino	Μονόκλινο
double room	'diklino	Δίκλινο
key	kli'dhi	Κλειδί
room card	ilektronni'ko kli'dhi	Ηλεκτρονικό κλειδί

HEALTH

doctor/dentist/ paediatrician	ya'tros/odhondoya'tros/ pe'dhiatros	Ιατρός/Οδοντογιατρός/ Παιδίατρος
hospital/ emergency clinic	nossoko'mio/ yatri'ko 'kentro	Νοσοκομείο/ Ιατρικό κέντρο
fever/pain	piret'tos/'ponnos	Πυρετός/Πόνος
diarrhoea/nausea	dhi'arria/ana'gula	Διάρροια/Αναγούλα
sunburn	ilia'ko 'engavma	Ηλιακό έγκαυμα
inflamed/ injured	molli'menno/ pligo'menno	μολυμένο /πληγωμένο
pain reliever/tablet	paf'siponna/'chapi	Παυσίπονο/Χάπι

USEFUL PHRASES

POST, TELECOMMUNICATIONS & MEDIA

stamp/letter	gramma'tossimo/'gramma	Γραμματόσημο/Γράμμα
postcard	kartpos'tall	Καρτ-ποστάλ
I need a landline phone card	kri'azomme 'mia tile'karta ya dhi'mossio tilefoni'ko 'thalamo	Χρειάζομαι μία τηλεκάρτα για δημόσιο τηλεφωνικό θάλαμο
I'm looking for a prepaid card for my mobile	tha 'ithella 'mia 'karta ya to kinni'to mu	Θα ήθελα μία κάρτα για το κινητό μου
Where can I find internet access?	pu bor'ro na vro 'prosvassi sto índernett?	Που μπορώ να βρω πρόσβαση στο ίντερνετ;
socket/adapter/charger	'briza/an'dapporras/fortis'tis	πρίζα/αντάπτορας/φορτιστής
computer/battery/rechargeable battery	ippologis'tis/batta'ria/eppanaforti'zomenni batta'ria	Υπολογιστής/μπαταρία/επαναφορτιζόμενη μπαταρία
internet connection/wifi	'sindhessi se as'sirmato 'dhitio/vaifai	Σύνδεση σε ασύρματο δίκτυο/WiFi

LEISURE, SPORTS & BEACH

beach	para'lia	Παραλία
sunshade/lounger	om'brella/ksap'plostra	Ομπρέλα/Ξαπλώστρα

NUMBERS

0	mi'dhen	μηδέν
1	'enna	ένα
2	'dhio	δύο
3	'tria	τρία
4	'tessera	τέσσερα
5	'pende	πέντε
6	'eksi	έξι
7	ef'ta	εφτά
8	och'to	οχτώ
9	e'nea	εννέα
10	'dhekka	δέκα
11	'endhekka	ένδεκα
12	'dodhekka	δώδεκα
20	'ikossi	είκοσι
50	pen'inda	πενήντα
100	eka'to	εκατό
200	dhia'kossia	διακόσια
1000	'chilia	χίλια
10000	'dhekka chil'iades	δέκα χιλιάδες

NOTES

MARCO POLO TRAVEL GUIDES

MARCO POLO

With ROAD ATLAS & PULL-OUT MAP

LAKE GARDA

BALDO WITH MOUNTAIN BIKE
Malcesine takes bikes too

SSES" IN SALÓ
plate "Bacetti"

Travel with
Insider
Tips

MARCO POLO

With STREET ATLAS & PULL-OUT MAP

NEW YORK

OWS, WILD FLOWERS AND SKYSCRAPERS
chic: the High Line in Chelsea

ON CLOUD NINE
bar at 230 Fifth Street

Travel with
Insider
Tips

MARCO POLO

With ROAD ATLAS & PULL-OUT MAP

FRENCH RIVIERA
NICE, CANNES & MONACO

SPECTACULAR GRAND CANYON DU VERDON
Breath-taking scenery that takes some beating

SNIFFING THE AIR
The perfume manufacturers of Grasse

Travel with
Insider
Tips

www.marcopolouk.com

MARCO POLO

With ROAD ATLAS & PULL-OUT MAP

ALLORCA

EAN FLAIR IN THE MEDITERRANEAN
Mallorca's most beautiful beach

E IN" CROWD MEET
onda in Deià

Travel with
Insider
Tips

MARCO POLO

With STREET ATLAS & PULL-OUT MAP

BERLIN

A STUNNING ISLAND JUST FOR ART
Showcasing treasures from around the world

STAY COOL AT NIGHT
scene sets the trend

Travel with
Insider
Tips

- PACKED WITH INSIDER TIPS
- BEST WALKS AND TOURS
- FULL-COLOUR PULL-OUT MAP
  AND STREET ATLAS

ROAD ATLAS

The green line ▬▬ indicates the Trips & tours (p. 80–85)
The blue line ▬▬ indicates the Perfect route (p. 30–31)

All tours are also marked on the pull-out map

Photo: Sandy beach at Kamári south of Kéfalos

Exploring Kos

The map on the back cover shows how the area has been sub-divided

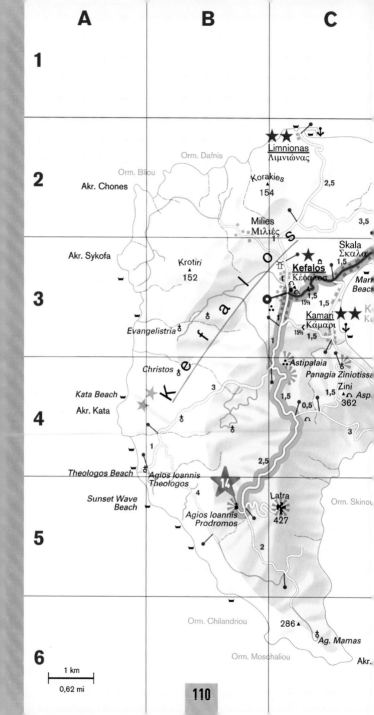

A   B   C

1

2

Orm. Dafnis

Orm. Bliou

Akr. Chones

★★
Limnionas
Λιμνιώνας

Korakies
154

2,5

3,5

Milies
Μιλιές

Akr. Sykofa

Krotiri
152

Skala
Σκάλα
1,5

★
Kefalos
Κέφαλος

Mar
Beac

15%   1,5

3

Evangelistria

Kamari
Κάμαρι

★★
K
Ke

15%   1,5

Christos

Astipalaia

Panagia Ziniotissa

Zini
362

Asp

Kata Beach
Akr. Kata

3

1,5

0,5

3

4

Theologos Beach
Sunset Wave
Beach

1

Agios Ioannis
Theologos

4

★14

Latra
427

2,5

Orm. Skinou

Agios Ioannis
Prodromos

2

5

Orm. Chilandriou

286

Ag. Mamas

Orm. Moschaliou

Akr.

6

1 km

0,62 mi

110

D

E

F

Kerula

▲78

Kakos
▲77

3 **1**

Ag. Ioan

Ellinika
Ελληνικά

Volkania
Βολκάνια

2

0,5

20
2,5

▲115

2

Ag. Georgios

▲79

Sunny
Beach

Polemi Beach
(Magic Beach)

Chrysi Akti
(Golden Beach)

4

2

Markos B.

Langada Beach

Paradise Beach ★★

Ag. Stefanos
Αγ. Στέφανος

▲63

Orm. Almyrou

Akr. Tigani

1

ri ★

Akr. Ag. Stefanos

Camel Beach

13

A I G A I O N

P E L A G O S **3**

'alou
αλου

4

Routhiano
Peli)

ama

A Ι Γ Α Ι Ο N

Π Ε Λ Α Γ Ο Σ

5

Mandraki

6

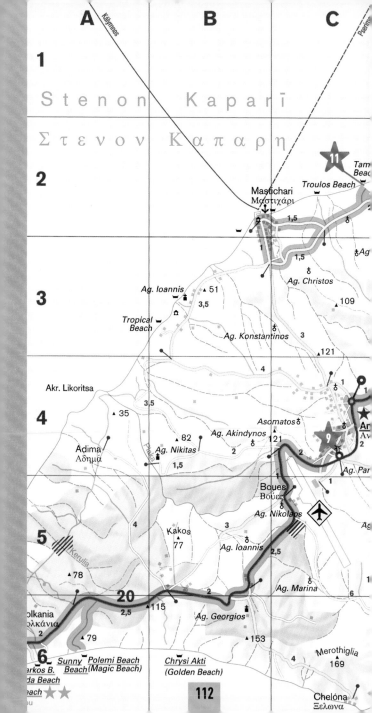

Stenon Kaparī

Στενον Καπαρη

A B C

1

2

Tam
Bead

11

Troulos Beach

Mastichari
Μαστιχάρι

1,5

1,5

Ag

Ag. Christos

Ag. Ioannis

▲ 51

3,5

Ag

Tropical
Beach

Ag. Konstantinos 3

109

▲121

3

Akr. Likoritsa

4

3,5

Asomatos

▲ 35

Ag. Akindynos

121

Ar
Αν

9

2

Adima
Αδημά

▲ 82

Plaka

Ag. Nikitas

2

1,5

Ag. Par

2

Boues
Βουές

Ag. Nikolaos

5

4

Kerulia

Kakos
77

3

Ag. Ioannis

2,5

Ag

▲ 78

2

Ag. Marina

6

olkania
ολκάνια
2

20

2,5

▲115

Ag. Georgios

▲ 79

▲153

Merothiglia
169

6

arkos B.

Sunny
Beach

Polemi Beach
(Magic Beach)

Chrysi Akti
(Golden Beach)

4

da Beach

each

★★

Chelóna
Ξελώνα

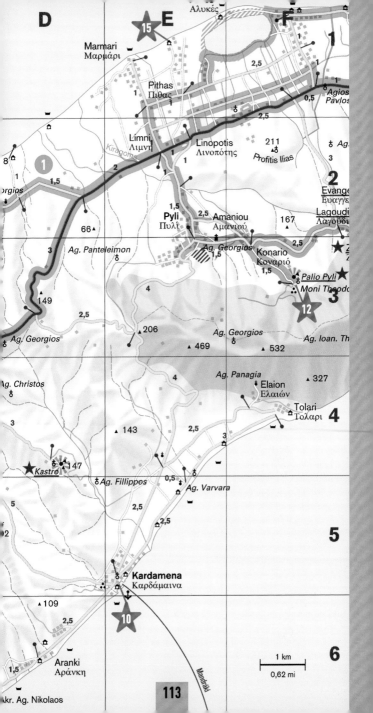

D

E

F

1

Αλυκές

Marmari
Μαρμάρι

15

Pithas
Πιθας

2,5

Agios
Pavlos

0,5

Limni
Λιμνη

Linopotis
Λινοπότης

Kiragoma

211

Profitis Ilias
Προφίτης Ηλίας

Ag.

3

2

1

orgios

1

1,5

2

1,5

1,5

66▲

Pyli
Πυλί

2,5

Amaniou
Αμανιού

167
▲

Evange
Ευαγγε

Lagoudi
Λαγούδι

Ag. Panteleimon

Ag. Georgios

1,5

Konario
Κονάριό

2,5

3

1,5

Palio Pyli

Moni Theoda

★

12

149

▲

2,5

4

3

Ag. Georgios

▲206

Ag. Georgios

▲469

▲532

Ag. Ioan. Th

Ag. Christos

4

Ag. Panagia

▲327

Elaion
Ελαιών

Tolari
Τολαρι

4

3

▲143

2,5

2

3

Kastro

147

Ag. Fillippos

0,5

Ag. Varvara

5

2,5

2

2,5

5

Kardamena
Καρδάμαινα

▲109

10

2,5

Mandraki

1 km

0,62 mi

6

1,5

Aranki
Αράνκη

113

kr. Ag. Nikolaos

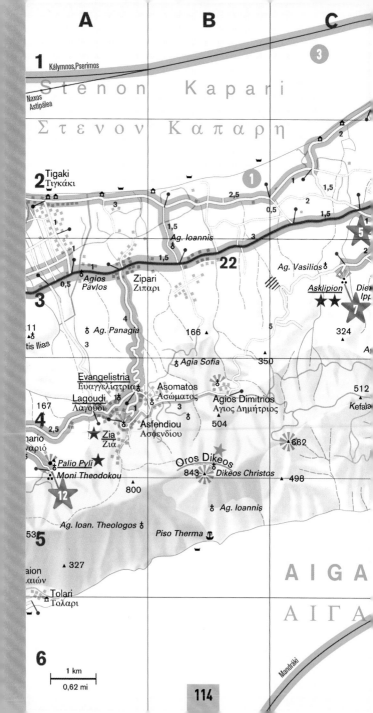

A

B

C

1 Kálymnos, Pserimos

Naxos
Astipálea

S t e n o n   K a p a r i

Σ τ ε ν ο ν   Κ α π α ρ η

2 Tigaki
Τιγκάκι

2,5

1,5

0,5

1,5

Ag. Ioannis

1,5

22

Ag. Vasilios

Asklipion

Dier
Ipp

5

7

324

3 Agios
Pavlos

Zipari
Ζιπαρι

0,5

.11

tis Ilias

4

Ag. Panagia

3

166 ▲

5

350

Ag. Ioannis

512

Kefala

Agia Sofia

Evangelistria
Ευαγγελιστρια

Lagoudi
Λαγούδι

4

167

2,5

nario
αριό

Zia
Ζιά

Asomatos
Ασώματος

3

Agios Dimitrios
Άγιος Δημήτριος

504

662

Palio Pyli

Moni Theodokou

12

800

Asfendiou
Ασφενδίου

Oros Dikeos

843 ▲

Dikeos Christos

▲ 498

Ag. Ioannis

Ag. Ioan. Theologos

Piso Therma

53

5

aion
αιών

▲ 327

A I G A

A I Γ A

Tolari
Τολαρι

Mandráki

6

1 km

0,62 mi

KEY TO ROAD ATLAS

Autobahn · Gebührenpflichtige Anschlussstelle · Gebührenstelle · Anschlussstelle mit Nummer · Rasthaus mit Übernachtung · Raststätte · Kleinraststätte · Tankstelle · Parkplatz mit und ohne WC	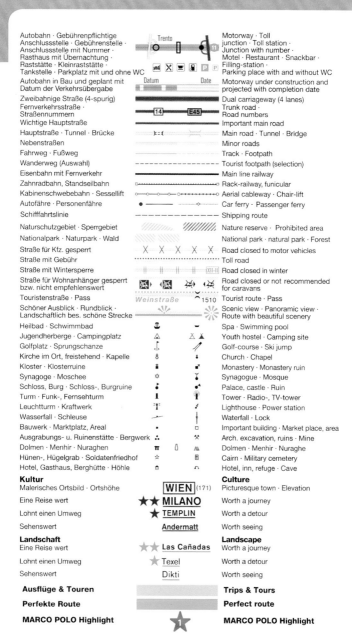	Motorway · Toll junction · Toll station · Junction with number · Motel · Restaurant · Snackbar · Filling-station · Parking place with and without WC
Autobahn in Bau und geplant mit Datum der Verkehrsübergabe	Datum · Date	Motorway under construction and projected with completion date
Zweibahnige Straße (4-spurig)		Dual carriageway (4 lanes)
Fernverkehrsstraße · Straßennummern	14 · E45	Trunk road · Road numbers
Wichtige Hauptstraße		Important main road
Hauptstraße · Tunnel · Brücke		Main road · Tunnel · Bridge
Nebenstraßen		Minor roads
Fahrweg · Fußweg		Track · Footpath
Wanderweg (Auswahl)		Tourist footpath (selection)
Eisenbahn mit Fernverkehr		Main line railway
Zahnradbahn, Standseilbahn		Rack-railway, funicular
Kabinenschwebebahn · Sessellift		Aerial cableway · Chair-lift
Autofähre · Personenfähre		Car ferry · Passenger ferry
Schifffahrtslinie		Shipping route
Naturschutzgebiet · Sperrgebiet		Nature reserve · Prohibited area
Nationalpark · Naturpark · Wald		National park · natural park · Forest
Straße für Kfz. gesperrt	X X X X X	Road closed to motor vehicles
Straße mit Gebühr		Toll road
Straße mit Wintersperre	XII-II	Road closed in winter
Straße für Wohnanhänger gesperrt bzw. nicht empfehlenswert		Road closed or not recommended for caravans
Touristenstraße · Pass	Weinstraße · 1510	Tourist route · Pass
Schöner Ausblick · Rundblick · Landschaftlich bes. schöne Strecke		Scenic view · Panoramic view · Route with beautiful scenery
Heilbad · Schwimmbad		Spa · Swimming pool
Jugendherberge · Campingplatz		Youth hostel · Camping site
Golfplatz · Sprungschanze		Golf-course · Ski jump
Kirche im Ort, freistehend · Kapelle		Church · Chapel
Kloster · Klosterruine		Monastery · Monastery ruin
Synagoge · Moschee		Synagogue · Mosque
Schloss, Burg · Schloss-, Burgruine		Palace, castle · Ruin
Turm · Funk-, Fernsehturm		Tower · Radio-, TV-tower
Leuchtturm · Kraftwerk		Lighthouse · Power station
Wasserfall · Schleuse		Waterfall · Lock
Bauwerk · Marktplatz, Areal		Important building · Market place, area
Ausgrabungs- u. Ruinenstätte · Bergwerk		Arch. excavation, ruins · Mine
Dolmen · Menhir · Nuraghen	π · Ո · ⚲	Dolmen · Menhir · Nuraghe
Hünen-, Hügelgrab · Soldatenfriedhof	☆ · ⊞	Cairn · Military cemetery
Hotel, Gasthaus, Berghütte · Höhle		Hotel, inn, refuge · Cave

Kultur		**Culture**
Malerisches Ortsbild · Ortshöhe	WIEN (171)	Picturesque town · Elevation
Eine Reise wert	★★ MILANO	Worth a journey
Lohnt einen Umweg	★ TEMPLIN	Worth a detour
Sehenswert	Andermatt	Worth seeing
Landschaft		**Landscape**
Eine Reise wert	★★ Las Cañadas	Worth a journey
Lohnt einen Umweg	★ Texel	Worth a detour
Sehenswert	Dikti	Worth seeing

Ausflüge & Touren		**Trips & Tours**
Perfekte Route		**Perfect route**
MARCO POLO Highlight	⭐	**MARCO POLO Highlight**

INDEX

All the places, islands and destinations for trips mentioned in the book are listed in this index. Bold figures refer to the main entry.

WRITE TO US

e-mail: info@marcopologuides.co.uk

Did you have a great holiday?
Is there something on your mind?
Whatever it is, let us know!
Whether you want to praise, alert us
to errors or give us a personal tip –
MARCO POLO would be pleased to
hear from you.
We do everything we can to provide
the very latest information for your trip.

Nevertheless, despite all of our authors'
thorough research, errors can creep
in. MARCO POLO does not accept any
liability for this. Please contact us by
e-mail or post.

MARCO POLO Travel Publishing Ltd
Pinewood, Chineham Business Park
Crockford Lane, Chineham
Basingstoke, Hampshire RG24 8AL
United Kingdom

PICTURE CREDITS
Cover image: Sporadhes Island (Getty Images/Robert Harding World Imagery: I Openers)
Photos: K. Bötig (1 bottom); DuMont picture archive: Kiedrowski (94); Grecotel S.A. (2 centre, top, 9, 47); Getty Images/Robert Harding World Imagery: I Openers (1 top); R. Hackenberg (flap r., 7, 41, 49, 50, 51, 63, 64/65, 77); Huber: Johanna Huber (98 top), Huber (12/13), Müller-St. (95), Schmid (3 o., 3 centre bottom, 8, 10/11, 18/19, 38/39, 42/43, 68, 70/71, 78/79, 80/81), Giovanni Simeone (flap left, 2 centre bottom, 15, 26 r., 32/33, 34); F. Ihlow (23, 30 l., 36, 56/57); International Health Film Festival: Vassia Anagnostopoulou (17 top); R. Irek (85, 98 bottom); © iStockphoto.com: maria bacarella (17 bottom), James Pauls (16 centre.), Vernon Wiley (16 top); Laif: Caputo (26 l.), IML (3 u., 86/87, 99), Zanettini (93); E. Laue (2 bottom, 30 r., 52/53, 61, 75); Look: Jorda (89), Pompe (2 top, 4, 29, 72), van Dierendonck (5); mauritius images: Clasen (45), Habel (59, 108/109), Jiri (27, 54), Plant (6), Waldkirch (28/29), World Pictures (28), Zak (20); M. Pasdzior (67); S. Randebrock (24/25); T. Stankiewicz (83, 90/91); K. -Thiele (94/95); WEST Bar (16 bottom)

1st Edition 2012
Worldwide Distribution: Marco Polo Travel Publishing Ltd, Pinewood, Chineham Business Park,
Crockford Lane, Basingstoke, Hampshire RG24 8AL, United Kingdom. Email: sales@marcopolouk.com
© MAIRDUMONT GmbH & Co. KG, Ostfildern
Editor in chief: Michaela Lienemann (concept, managing editor), Marion Zorn (concept, text editor)
Author: Klaus Bötig, editor: Wieland Höhne
Programme supervision: Ann-Katrin Kutzner, Nikolai Michaelis, Silwen Randebrock
Picture editor: Wieland Höhne, Gabriele Forst
What's hot: wunder media, Munich; Cartography road atlas: © MAIRDUMONT, Ostfildern
Cartography pull-out map: © MAIRDUMONT, Ostfildern
Design: milchhof : atelier, Berlin; Front cover, pull-out map cover, page 1: factor product munich
Translated from German by Kathleen Becker, Lisbon; editor of the English edition: John Sykes, Cologne
Phrase book in cooperation with Ernst Klett Sprachen GmbH, Stuttgart, Editorial by Pons Wörterbücher

DOS & DON'TS

A few things you should bear in mind on Kos

ANCIENT SOUVENIRS

The Greeks would like to hang on to their antiquities. This means that at ancient sites it is prohibited to as much as pick up a shard of pottery.

A CHEAPIE BODRUM TRIP

At the harbour you can pick up a ticket for a trip across to Turkey for as little as 10 euros, including a guided tour of the town. The problem here: the tour leads mainly to carpet dealers and shopping centres, where the promoter pockets high commissions.

SNAPPING AWAY WITHOUT ASKING

Many Greeks have no problem having their photograph taken, but do object to holidaymakers acting like hunters. Before pressing the button, check with a little smile that your subject is happy to be photographed.

LIGHTING A FIRE

There is a great danger of forest fires in Kos. Smokers therefore are asked to be particularly careful. A cigarette butt, carelessly thrown away, can trigger a disaster.

BUYING BAD ICONS

Instead of insisting on 'real' icons that have merely been made to look like antiques, buy new ones in the workshop of the local painter of icons.

IGNORING TRAFFIC REGULATIONS

Greek traffic penalties can be eye-watering. Parking in the wrong place entails a fine of 60 euros, running a red light 700 euros.

SLIPPING AND SLIDING

Even on short hikes: wear at least trainers, no sandals. The paths are often rocky and slippery. Also, there are snakes. They might be rare and won't look for confrontations, but you never know.

DISTURBING GREEK SIESTAS

Many Greeks observe a siesta between 2 and 6pm. Make sure you keep your private calls for outside those hours.

ORDERING FISH UNSEEN

In Greece, fresh fish is sold at exorbitant prices, and often by weight. Ask for the kilo price and try to be present when it's being weighed too, to avoid unpleasant surprises.

HIRING A CAR WITHOUT COMPARING PRICES

With rental cars, it is well worth comparing prices. Hire car firms often pay commissions to hotels and tour guides; it is best to check with the hire car companies direct.